Memoirs as History: Contextualizing Bengal

Editors
Pradip Chattopadhyay
Aparajita Dhar
Binata Sarkar

Setu Prakashani
In association with
the Department of History
The University of Burdwan

Memoirs as History: Contextualizing Bengal
Editors
Pradip Chattopadhyay
Aparajita Dhar
Binata Sarkar

1st Edition : January 2022

ISBN : 978-81-953908-0-9
Cover : Dilip Ghosh

Published by
Archana Das & Subrata Das
on behalf of
Setu Prakashani
12 / A Shankar Ghosh Lane, Kolkata-6
Phone : +91 33 2219 0704, +91 94330 74548
In association with
the Department of History
The University of Burdwan

Outlet:
2, Shyama Charan Dey Street, Kolkata- 700 073
'Bookmark', 6 Bankim Chatterjee Street, Kolkata- 700 073
e-mail : setuprakashani@gmail.com
Website : www.setuprakashani.com

Price: Rupees Two hundred Twenty Five

Compose by Cynosure, 26, Jodhpur Garden, Kolkata - 45
Printed by Imprinta, 243/2B APC Road, Kolkata-6

Contents

century, the scope for searching a new set of sources other than the conventional ones and the concern for language and readability aspect of historical writing took a backseat during this period. The debate continued unabated throughout the nineteenth and twentieth centuries only to redefine the interrelationship between history, science and literature. In the milieu opinions regarding the choice of sources and approaches to writing history have undergone changes. Gradually recognition came for looking into new set of sources as well as for exploring newer approaches to search historical truth and objectivity. These factors are commonly believed to have rendered the art of writing history a state of perfection of what it is today.

In recent years, however, scholars of India as well as those of the Middle East and South East Asia have begun to reject the idea that a developed sense of selfhood has existed only in the west. Written texts primarily biographies and autobiographies, as well as personal memoirs are viewed as valuable sources for understanding the emergence of a modern sense of self, of individualism and self-consciousness as opposed to collective identity, and or a constant interaction and negotiation between the two. These enable us to understand more intelligibly the complex forces at work in modern societies and to reflect further and from more solid foundations on many of the major themes that dominate the subcontinent— gender, modernity, colonialism and nationalism, religion, social change, family and kinship and interrelationship between self and society. There has been a move away from the polished biographies and autobiographies of the 'great and famous' toward the investigation of more marginalized and subaltern sections of society. A growing distrust for meta-narratives, a new found skepticism toward sweeping generalizations and grand theories of social change and hence a move toward a more nuanced, multi-stranded approach to understand society and a greater recognition of the heterogeneity of

Editor's Note

Memoirs as History: Contextualizing Bengal

There is little doubt that the art of history writing has evolved much over the centuries and has achieved to an agreeable degree a state of perfection in recent times. The inter-disciplinary character of history is evident since inception through its affiliation with philosophy and literature in the past. However, the attempt to redefine the frontiers and the methodology of history writing by scholars as great as Niebuhr, Ranke, Toynbee, Braudel and others has rendered it an altogether new character hitherto unprecedented in western historical tradition. Earlier, government documents or those preserved in archives were regarded as infallible for writing histories of different countries particularly when Rankean philosophy of writing empirical history ruled the roost in the nineteenth century. The other variety of sources such as oral evidences, private diaries, autobiographies, biographies, memoirs, folk tales, etc., have suffered a neglect as a result and hardly received due attention from scholars as valid sources of history. The limitation thrust upon the choice of sources was further compounded by the development of the debate whether history could be called a science and that a proper scientific methodology was necessary to write history. Thus while searching historical truth and objectivity became the soul passion of historians to write histories in the nineteenth human lives and lived experience have become the staple of history writing in present times.

In his famous essay, 'Post Coloniality and the Artifice of History', Dipesh Chakraborty points out that with the emergence of many of the public and private rituals of modern life in nineteenth century India, there was a sudden efflorescence of four basic literary genres which helped express the modern self :- the novel, the biography, the autobiography and history. This was particularly true for colonial Bengal which witnessed a tremendous growth of personal narratives including autobiography, memoirs and reminiscences that acted as primary vehicles for articulating middle class identity and revealing the rich matrix of the colonial households and the society at large.

Biographies, autobiographies and memoirs have always been assigned an important place in Indian historical tradition. Since history was enmeshed with literature and no strict segregation between history and literature was thought of in the past, good biographies, as a branch of literature were written based on the events and ideas of the contemporary period. These narratives contain enough historical materials to reckon with. Even today odd variants of literature such as myths, fables, fictions biographies or memoirs etc., were considered to be a part of historical literature as they contain valuable sources of information for reconstruction of the past. While the historical value of information derived from such sources is a subject of intense debate and remains open to be challenged by scholars across the disciplines, some scholars have tended to characterize them as 'quasi history' and therefore not totally redundant. Still others, such as Satish Chandra Mitra, D.D. Koshambi have openly defended their importance on the ground that such sources often turn out to be valuable in shedding light on the histories of certain obscure periods or of unknown or little-known communities having obscure origin and activities remaining far away from the focus of mainstream life. Thus despite being historical sources of different category their potential cannot be underestimated or needs to be reviewed owing to the development of a totally new genre of history writing in recent times in the form of subaltern history, regional history or village histories. In this context, biographies, autobiographies annals, memoirs etc., exhibit as much legitimacy as sources for writing history as archival sources.

The proposed edited volume therefore aims at proving a point that biographies, autobiographies and memoirs of people are important sources in their own right since they significantly contribute to our understanding of past historical moments. The volume is based on a collection of essays/articles presented in the seminar entitled Autobiography, Biography and Memoirs as History: Contextualizing Bengal. The heterogeneity of themes in the volume however does not undermine the basic unity of narrative in exposing the diverse strands and discourses on modernity. The following is an overview of the themes presented by scholars in their respective papers.

Section-II

Sreelata Chatterjee, in her essay, entitled 'Hospitals in Urban Biography: Public Health and Foundation of Hospitals in Early Colonial Calcutta 1707-1854' has tried to analyze the foundation of hospitals in the evolution of municipal and public health system in the urban biography of Calcutta in between the period 1707 and 1854. She has argued that hospital development in Calcutta was closely linked to the city's changing environment shaped as much by the forces of colonialism as by the internal dynamics of social change within the city. While the first section of her essay examines the development of military hospitals for the Europeans in Calcutta the second section aims at showing how the process of urbanization brought about a change in the earlier enclavist military medical policy to the acceptance of wider public health measures.

Aparna Bandyopadhyay in her paper entitled, 'A History of Intimacy through Women's Self-Writings in Colonial Bengal' seeks to unravel the predicament of unhappy wives and widows as revealed in their diaries, the latter being used as a veritable source of constructing the history of intimate conjugal relations in colonial Bengal. A diary although recorded the author's experiences, emotions and sensibilities on a day to day basis was not intended for publication and therefore developed as the most personal form of self-revelation. Prof. Bandyopadhyay delves into the diaries left behind by women like Amiyabala, Subarnaprabha Das, Priyangbada Devi, Nirupama Devi and others and attempts to arrive through these articulations at a more nuanced understanding of women's intimate lives in colonial Bengal.

The article of Sahara Ahmed entitled, 'Green Regimes and Colonial Pasts: Vignettes of Botanical Garden and Histories of Marginalised People, c. 1890-1970' primarily focuses on upholding biographies and memoirs of both the European and Indian writers as important sources for understanding the European perspective of operation and management of scientific forestry on the one hand and the stories of struggle and discrimination of Indian forest dwellers on the other. The essay has been divided into two sections with two distinct arguments to follow. The first section is devoted to highlight the emergence of scientific forestry and its rational management in the form of emergence of Botanical garden in Calcutta where questions as intriguing as the imposition of European notion of proprietary rights on land and labour and the commercial interest of the Company in the formulation of such policy have been addressed. The second section emphatically deals with stories of eviction of forest dwellers and their exploitation and discrimination in the hands of colonial masters which in many cases forced them to craft alternative strategies of survival. Weaving through memoirs the second part of this paper probes into a multiplicity of forest lives trajectories and struggles in the Jalpaiguri district with the onset of colonial intervention.

The article of Arpita Bose entitled, 'A Short Biography of Tan-Yunshan: Retrieving from Archival Documents' explores the different facts of the contribution of Tanyun Shan in India. His role in building Cheena Bhavan at Viswa-Bharati Santiniketan and in developing Sino-Indian cultural ties in the decades following the Second World War have been brought to light with great emphasis. The author here has particularly dealt with his life and career, how it evolved over the decades marked by deep-seated intellectual influence of Rabindranath Tagore on him that inspired him to visit India repeatedly and build Cheena Bhavan at Viswa-Bharati Santiniketan where he took the job of teaching. Reference has also been made to his political ideology and shifting loyalties from Chinese Kuomintang party to People's Republic of China and the role he played as a cultural ambassador of China in India. Among other issues his relationship with Indian intellectuals and political leaders of independent India and his role in the development of Sino-Indian relationship both at times of trouble and peace in the aftermath of Indian independence have been discussed at length.

Sumita Chakraborty's article entitled, 'Inter-relation between History & Biography: Exploring Nineteenth Century History in Sivnath Sashtri's Biography Ramtanu Lahiri O Tatkalin Banga Samaj' seeks to explore the importance of biography in understanding the socio-cultural matrix of the nineteenth century. The author has tried to understand the nuances of the history of Bengal Renaissance from the perspective of a Brahmo reformer namely Sivnath Shastri who in his writing Ramtanu Lahiri O Tatkalin Banga Samaj has put together many known and unknown events of nineteenth century Bengal. The transformation that was taking place in many Bengali families during this time owing to their shift to Calcutta for availing better opportunities of job and education in colonial Calcutta has well been addressed in this essay. In addition to these the historical forces, factors and figures believed to have played decisive roles in bringing cultural resurgence in nineteenth century Calcutta have been highlighted in the article with merit.

The article of Bidisha Chakroborty entitled, 'Reflection of Rural Crime and Control in Memoirs and Biographies' seeks to explore the importance of biographies, autobiographies and memoirs in highlighting the declining situation of law and order in rural Bengal during the early years of Company's rule in Bengal. There is little doubt that the second half of the eighteenth century witnessed a process of transition from Nawabi Bengal to colonial Bengal. The advent of the British witnessed the breakdown of the old system and the resultant displacement of authority in the Bengal Subah. Historical sources like diaries, memoirs and biographies not only throw ample light on the causes, context and major players of rural crime but also provide us with alternative accounts on them totally unavailable in government documents. The gaps existing in the public records can be filled-in through these sources and the narratives that surface in such personal reminisces are historically worthwhile to study.

Debraj Chakraborty's essay 'Representation of Birds in the Jahangirnama: Narratives and Visuals' portrays a fascinating tale on the natural world of medieval India with special emphasis on birds and other living organisms of the wild life of those days. Based on contemporary sources, miniatures and other paintings as well as travelogues the essay represents the approach of the Mughal emperors towards animal life, especially birds. The scholar has effectively traced in the article the interest of Mughal rulers in birds particularly in their ways of mating and several other odd behaviours being watched by emperors with keen interest as avid lovers of wild life. In the process the rulers represented themselves not only as the patrons of the animal world but combined in them the rare attributes of a naturalist, ornithologist and animal lover alongside being deft conquerors and administrators. The fascination for natural flora and fauna of medieval India has been expressed in no uncertain terms by Babur himself in his biography and the legacy of writing on the natural world thus set was further carried forward by Jahangir and others in the subsequent years.

Nirmal Bandopadhyay, in his article, 'Reflections on History, Nation and Gender in Binodini Dasi's Autobiography: *Amar Katha*' shows how with the introduction of actresses in public theatre in the 1870s, a new dimension was added to Bengali society. On the basis of Binodini Dasi's autobiography *Amar Katha*, the author points out that the representation of women as public performers would have undermined the cultural project of the educated middle class as the female performers hailed from the strata of prostitutes. Although theatre acted as a site of work and a source of livelihood the social reformers in their agenda for women had remained conspicuously silent on this section of women. Binodini Dasi's life as a professional actress was thus marked by varied contradictions of the new world of middle class cultural production.

Hospitals in Urban Biography: Public Health and Foundation of Hospitals in Early Colonial Calcutta (1707-1854)

Srilata Chatterjee

Urban biography has emerged as an important field of study narrating the historical process of urbanization of a city in its varied aspects. In this paper an attempt has been made to trace the foundation of hospitals in the evolution of municipal and public health system in the urban biography of Calcutta.[1] The period of study spans from 1707 till 1854 that is early colonial period.

Researches on urban history of Calcutta have primarily dealt with the social process of urban development with little emphasis on public health, sanitation and medical administration.[2] In recent years however an attempt has been made to link Calcutta's town planning with hospital development and public health.[3] Focusing on the role of James Ranald Martin, a Scottish medical practitioner in Calcutta and his study of the Medical Topography of Calcutta, Partho Datta argues that a 'new notion of public that of public health in Calcutta' was created by Martin. His endeavour led to the establishment of new hospitals but it also resulted in the state withdrawing from medical charity to engage in reforms like public health which proved ruinous for the public.[4] Drawing from these studies this paper will try to argue that hospital development in Calcutta was closely linked to the city's changing environment shaped as much by forces of colonialism as by the internal dynamics of social change within the city. This paper is divided into two sections. The first section examines the development of military hospitals for the Europeans in Calcutta. The second section aims to show how the process of urbanization brought about a change in the earlier enclavist military medical policy to the acceptance of wider public health measures.

The European Enclave: Military Hospitals in Early Colonial Calcutta

The city of Calcutta represents a development wherein a riverine aggregate of rural settlements grew into an urban centre as an outcome of colonial commercial and political activities. While politically and strategically Calcutta was well suited to be an administrative and commercial capital, Calcutta's insalubrious climate was a cause of concern for the European settlers of the city. The choice of Calcutta by Charnock as a site for the British factory was regarded as unfortunate for 'he could not have chosen a more unhealthful place on the entire river.'[5] The salt water lake, situated three miles to the northeast of Calcutta was seen as the main source of putrid sinking vapors which caused yearly mortality of the Europeans.[6] The climatic considerations of wind direction, impact of heat and humidity on health and the general topography of the land along with commercial and political factors were given primacy in constructing early hospitals under the East India Company.

The first hospital that was established in Calcutta was a fort hospital situated within Fort William primarily to serve the military medical needs of the Company. But it was destroyed in 1756 during the siege of Calcutta by Siraj-ud-Daulah, the Nawab of Bengal along with many other buildings.[7] The need for a general hospital for the Europeans arose because the second temporarily improvised hospital within the fort did not cater to the large number of European civilians living in the city. The European civil population in Calcutta was increasing and comprised the more affluent Europeans engaged in the Company's service or other kinds of successful professions and also a considerable number of poor and marginal Europeans. While the affluent Europeans at the higher stratum of social order lived in the white town, the poorer Europeans including Portuguese and Armenians were forced to inhabit the fringes of the European quarters. They lived in conditions of squalor and poverty which made them an easy prey to illness and they needed hospital care far more than the established Europeans who could have arranged treatment at home. Secondly once Calcutta's importance as a port increased, it became necessary to create institutional care for the mariners visiting the city. In the eighteenth century amongst several General Hospitals that were set up to take care of the medical needs of the army, the Presidency General Hospital was established in Calcutta to treat the European civilians and sailors. This was the first attempt to break away from the limited goal of providing only for medical needs of the army and taking care of the health of the European population residing in various parts of the city. The Presidency General Hospital came up as a single in-house hospital outside the fortified area. It was placed under the Hospital Board after its creation in 1786 with a set of medical regulations to control its functioning.[8]

The Presidency General Hospital was predominantly a military hospital but it was also an institution of medical charity and welfare treating homeless and indigent Europeans in the city free of cost. Patients were admitted on recommendations from Government officials. Unlike the Madras General Hospital which admitted Indians from 1842, the Presidency General Hospital maintained its racial segregation and military character well into the nineteenth century. There is no denying the fact that the European hospital symbolized the process of militarization of medical care in the European quarters, yet often in its internal functioning the hospital failed to emulate the discipline and rationalization of European military hospitals. Military needs dominated over needs of humane care. There were serious allegations against the hospital that the soldiers were being released before they recovered from their illness. John Barrow and Francis Deeds, both of them Privates in the 17th regiment, had complained that they were discharged so weak and debilitated that they were unable to discharge their duties for a considerable time.[9] In British India army hospitals like the Presidency General developed as an institution of imperial power and domination through a process of segregation and militarization of European hospitals.[10] The importance of hospitals as institutions of human care and cure was subsumed by their position within the hierarchically dominated British military medical administration which often created resentment even among the European medical practitioners of the city.[11]

Public Health and Hospitals for the 'Natives'

As the urban area in Calcutta began to expand and there was greater social and occupational interaction between the Europeans and the local people, a more aggressive sanitation and municipal policy was implemented by the colonial state. The process began from 1794 with the formation of the Committee of Justices of Peace and afterwards the Lottery Committee. This initiated an era of municipal sanitation through organized committees, public subscription thus transplanting in the opinion of Goode the English institutional model onto Indian soil.[12]

This was also the time when new theories of medical geography began to influence the European settlers in the Tropics which involved finding the causal relation between environment, climate and disease. The medico-climatic discourse which began to take shape from this time attributed the dynamism and progress of the Europeans and their racial superiority to the cooler climate of the temperate zone and identified the tropical lands with natural fecundity and rapid decay. Diseases in the tropics were associated closely with the hot and humid climate and the miasma or putrid vapour from decaying organic matters.[13] Much of this knowledge was constructed by the doctors in the Medical Service which on one hand brought up the issue of European acclimatization to diverse local conditions, on the other it created an urge amongst the medical practitioners to find the natural locus of tropical diseases among the local population. A special knowledge about the medical topography of the tropical lands also proved professionally beneficial to the European practitioners of the Indian Medical Service in securing their position within the medical hierarchy. In the late eighteenth century the IMS doctors acted as negotiators inducing the early colonial state to take some interest in matters other than military and politics.

In Calcutta the first dispensary system of hospital for the 'natives' was established primarily to treat surgical cases of accidents. The Native General Hospital and its dispensaries in Park Street, Dharmatulla and Guranhatta were founded in 1792 on the initiative of Dr. Robert Wilson, a member of the Medical Board and through public meetings of the European residents of the city because,

> The want of a hospital or institution for the relief of persons suffering from accidents being severely felt by the native inhabitants of Calcutta in general and more particularly by the labouring part of them, a plan for establishing such an institution as may be best calculated to afford relief ...

The hospital was run by a Trustee Committee appointed to receive subscriptions, draw a plan for the management of the hospital and also to convince the colonial state for aid. This financial patronage came in the form of a monthly charity of Rs. 600/ allocated to the Committee by the Collector of Behar drawn from the amount of duties collected from the pilgrims of Gayah.[15] But the Native Hospital which started in a rented house of the Faujdar of Chitpore was sustained financially through medical charity coming initially from Europeans and then from Indian elite. Although intended as a surgical hospital, it was forced to treat patients with varied ailments. The eighteenth century hospitals developing as a part of the municipal and town planning process of the imperial capital actually provided the medical practitioners of the city first hand clinical experience of the etiology of tropical diseases among the local population and their cure through hospital care.

By early nineteenth century concerns to improve the condition of the city with regard to health and sanitation was getting expressed in the official exchanges. In 1803 Governor General Wellesley declared:

> The increasing extent and population of Calcutta, the capital of the British Empire in India and the seat of Supreme authority requires the serious attention of the Government. It has now become absolutely necessary to provide permanent means of promoting the health, comfort and convenience of the numerous inhabitants of this town.[16]

A Special Committee was appointed for improving the city to consider 'the existing nuisances in the town of Calcutta and proposing the best means of removing them.'[17] The primary aim was to create a city which would reflect the power of the Raj. In the process of creating an imperial urban culture, considerations of sanitation and public health for the first time was taken up by the government.

The nineteenth century also saw the outbreak of major epidemic diseases in the city of Calcutta and its suburbs which could be another cause of concern for the bureaucrats. In 1817 an epidemic of cholera in the city brought out the defects in the municipal administration and the failure of western medicine to control the disease. Native physicians had to be appointed to control the epidemic with local remedies. The general cause of the disease was thought to be extreme humidity, but official reports showed that the 'general cause was heightened by local causes the most important of which was drainage and lack of free ventilation in the town and its surroundings.'[18] The worst hit parts of the town were Burra bazaar, Mochoa bazaar, Simlya and in the suburbs Entally, Kidderpore, Bhowanipore, Manicktollah, Chitpore and Sealdah, the entire region being inhabited by the local population and low Europeans. The second was an outbreak of fever in 1833 mostly in the suburbs of Calcutta due to heavy rainfall and inundation in the previous years.[19]

Medical Topography of Calcutta and James Ranald Martin

It is within this context of debates on urban health and sanitation in the nineteenth century that the Medical Topography on Calcutta by James Ranald Martin and also his activities surrounding the committee to form a fever hospital needs to be situated. James Ranald Martin was a Scottish Surgeon in the service of the Company and was attached to the Native General Hospital in 1836 when he wrote 'Notes on Medical Topography of Calcutta'. Medical topographies emerged as a definite genre of scientific writing in India from the eighteenth century but in the wake of utilitarian reformism the writing of Medical Topographies also underwent a change. These new studies combined utilitarian reforms with theories of acclimatization.[20] It was claimed that European racial difference made biological acclimatization to the tropical landscape absolutely impossible. Therefore they advocated greater interventionist and aggressive administrative policies to reform the landscape to enhance its salubrity.

In opposition to contagion theories of the metropolitan scientists, medical practitioners in India were keenly promoting the environmental and miasmatic theory so that disease could be located in the landscape and not in the body. Martin in his medical topography propounded that all prevailing diseases could be related to some general external factors.

A knowledge of external circumstances which influence the health of the inhabitants of any particular country consciously designated Medical Topography when practically considered has for its objects the prevention of disease which in a large proportion of cases originates in external causes.[21]

Martin was extremely focused in his discussion of the Medical Topography for which he chose Calcutta, the epicenter of British Empire. Calcutta was also the place where as a practicing doctor in the Native Hospital, Martin had observed diseases most prevalent among local people. The city was important because in his view Calcutta took shape through British commerce and administration. He identified the city with British capital and enterprise so completely that the history before its reoccupation was considered as 'affording little promise of its future greatness.'[22] Martin attributed Calcutta's prosperity to the spirit of improvement in the years after Plassey in the following way,

> No where has the activity and enterprise of British commerce been better displayed than in the rapid rise of this capital. Previous to 1756 Calcutta was in short but a trading factory .... Soon after the reoccupation of Calcutta by the British an extraordinary impulse seems to have been given to

> the spirit of improvement, so that within forty years and notwithstanding all disadvantages of position, it became a city numbering five hundred thousand individuals, a degree of prosperity unparallel perhaps in any other quarter of the worlds.[23]

But Martin felt that sanitary and public health reforms in comparison to Calcutta's progress in urbanization were slow to develop especially in the Black Town. Sanitary reforms were more dependent on private speculators and enterprise which in course of time had ceased to operate. Under these circumstances, the paternalistic intervention of the government alone could prevent the city from decay, neglect and an unhealthy state.

Martin was focusing on a geographical location beyond the European quarters which had hitherto not been given much attention in the Medical Topographies by British medical practitioners. The native environment and habitation within the urban space was his point of reference and in this he was projecting the local population as the new 'public' whose health needed to be attended to.[24] The entire space outside the European habitation extending upto Chowringhee and inhabited by local people according to Martin was in a state of complete sanitary neglect and needed immediate refurbishing. Once again he claimed first hand experience as a doctor in the Native Hospital and also from his visits to houses of the local people. Here he could observe the etiology of fever in its natural form. Moreover such interactions with the local population helped him to develop his ideas about the disease and its relation with the environment. Of course he was extremely biased and racial in describing the Hindoo homes and cultural practices of the Bengali Baboo but was equally empathetic about the condition of the labouring poor of Calcutta.[25] Martin's Medical Topography delved into certain basic themes which included, the natural habitat of Calcutta and its demographic pattern, local people, their habitations and cultural practices along with descriptions about Calcutta climate and its impact on health, common diseases and their treatment in order to create a story of imperial Calcutta and its modes of control over ecological and geographical development. This paved the way for the formation of the Fever Hospital Committee for the establishment of a Fever Hospital in the city.

The Fever Hospital Committee and Background to the Foundation of the Medical College Hospital.

The Fever Hospital Committee which was initially formed at the independent initiative of the Governors of the Native Hospital especially James Ranald Martin through a public meeting held in the Town Hall also had indigenous elite as members. Dwarakanath Tagore, Rustomji Cowasji, Radhamadhab Banerjee, Ramcomul Sen, Muttylal Seal were invited to join the committee because 'it was thought right in the first instance to rely on them.'[26] These indigenous elite contributed large sums of money and also land for the construction of the hospital.[27] Hospitals emerged as new forms of civic philanthropy for the Indian elite towards the poor. Their attitude towards the poorer classes and response to public measures of sanitation apparently did not differ much from the British official attitude.. They too looked upon parts of the 'Native' town densely populated by the poorer class as source of all diseases and agreed that hospitals should develop through charity. In the committee's meeting Ramcomul Sen and Dr. Jackson jointly observed that,

> 'Of all charitable institutions, the establishment of hospitals for relief and preservation of health of the poor and infirm is of greatest benefit and utility, particularly in the metropolis like Calcutta to which people from every part of the city resort'.[28]

They intended hospitals to be built for the deprived and simultaneously were skeptic about the poorer classes availing the benefits of the hospital. Ramcomul Sen observed that people affected with fever were averse to accept relief provided with by the hospitals because of their habits, customs and religious scruples. He opined that these people would rather die in their huts and cottages because the hospital admitted indiscriminately all classes and castes of patients.[29] However, it can be argued that for many of these new elite who were in the forefront of social and economic transformation of nineteenth century Calcutta, the enthusiasm for urban health, sanitation and hospital development was also moulded by ideas of reform and progress towards western model of civic modernity.

The plan found favour with Lord Auckland primarily for two reasons, to aid medical education but more importantly because this plan would change the habits of the people injurious to their health. Under the Governor General's initiative the Committee was asked to deliberate with a holistic approach towards total improvement of the management of the town. The doctors who had earlier began with a plan of founding a disease specific institution now had to deal with a larger plan of improvement of the city involving local planned management and taxation for all matters connected with health and comfort. The issue of founding a fever hospital became linked to the wider plan of improvement of the city.

The Committee in its long deliberations and interviews with European and Indian practitioners in the town and also the indigenous elite concluded that the foundation of a central hospital capable of treating all kinds of diseases was an immediate need for the improvement of municipal and sanitary conditions of the city. Although Calcutta was the seat of government of the British Empire and an important trading centre, it did not have a hospital where people afflicted with disease like fever could be medically treated.[30] Growing emporia like Calcutta attracted a large number of people who came here in search of employment. Many of them engaged in menial professions lived with their fellow workers in congested surroundings. Such unhygienic living conditions made them prone to disease and in an unknown place when they were caught with fever or cholera, they had no means to procure medical aid. As their conditions worsened, they were often left to die without treatment or sent to their villages on a dooley, a journey they never survived.[31]

The Indian practitioners of western medicine like Madhusudan Gupta who were called upon to present before the Committee voiced a different concern which was related to the medicalisation of childbirth and reproductive health of the Hindu women. Madhusudan Gupta in his evidence stated that besides usual medical assistance given to men the Indian women should also get special attention during child-birth to prevent loss of life of the mother and the child. Hindu women who were married off at an early age suffered a great deal in parturition chiefly because of their young age. The most common cause was septic fever followed by lower abdominal pain and sweating. Madhusudan Gupta stated that,

> The symptoms could generally be prevented, if the woman was attended from the beginning by a skilful person. It would reduce infant mortality at birth and also the risks of childbirth for the mother. If a hospital with a lying–in ward was established with proper Hindoo midwives and attendants, a great number of married women of the inferior castes would be happy to avail them of it and many lives would be saved by this means.[32]

The Fever Hospital Committee initiated a new era in the history of public health and emphasized the need for a policy of institutional health care which would incorporate under the domain of public, the 'native' population of the town and their cultural habits and practices. This widening of the notion of 'public' also paved the way for the establishment of hospitals for the purpose of in house treatment culminating in the foundation of the Medical College Hospital in 1854 thereby providing the much needed institutional space through which western medicine would reach the city's inhabitants. The College Hospital was attached with the Medical College founded in 1835 to combine medical teaching with clinical observation for the benefit of students. By nineteenth century multiple systems of institutional medical care ranging from hospitals to scattered dispensaries, came into being as a part of the social process of Calcutta's urbanization and experiment in spatial management.

Conclusion

The foundation of the hospital system in Calcutta was closely linked to the growth of Calcutta as a colonial capital with a cosmopolitan culture. The political and social forces which were changing the city's socio-political and economic scenario from the nineteenth century also created a new public sphere where the colonizers and the elite among the colonized as reasoning public debated on issues of reform, progress and modernity. In this debate public health, sanitation and medicalisation of hospitals became important issues signifying modern urban development and creating a new notion of 'public' targeting the poor 'native' and their health. Hospitals that developed in Calcutta as a result of such utilitarian reformist intervention into the social space for urban improvement initiated a long experiment with public health blending the biological with social and transforming the environment of Calcutta's urban life.

Notes & References

1. This paper will deal with the development of general hospitals excluding Insane Hospitals for Europeans and 'Natives' and also the specialist hospitals whose development was not related to town planning and improvement scheme of the colonial government.
2. Sinha, Pradip, 'Calcutta in Urban History', in Chaudhuri Sukanta (ed.), *Calcutta e Living City*, Vol. 1, The Past, OUP,1990;
   Ray, A.K., *A Short History of Calcutta Town and its Suburbs*, Part I, (ed.) Nisith Ranjan Ray (Calcutta, 1982);
   Nisith Ranjan Roy, *Calcutta, the Profile of a City*, (K.P Bagchi, 1986);
   S.N Mukherjee, *Calcutta Essays in Urban History*, (Subarnarekha 1993);
   Swati Chattopadhyay, *Representing Calcutta: Modernity, Nationalism and the Colonial Uncanny 2005.*
3. Roy, Binay Bhusan, 'Native Haspatal Theke Fever Hospital', in Basu Debashis (ed.) *Kolkatar Purakatha*, Pustak Bipani, 1992, p?
4. Datta, Partho, 'Ranald Martin's Medical Topography (1837) The Emergence of Public Health in Calcutta' in Pati, Biswamoy and Harrison, Mark (ed.), *The Social History of Health and Medicine in Colonial Calcutta*, Primus Books, 2011, First published by Routledge, 2009, p. 15-30.
5. Hamilton, Alexander, 'A New Account of the East Indies', cited in, Nair, P.T., *Calcutta in the 18th Century: Impressions of Travellers*, Firma KLM Pvt. Ltd, Calcutta, 1984, pp. 4–5.
6. Ibid, p?
7. Fort William Public Consultation, October 16,1707, cited in Crawford, D.G., *The History of Indian Medical Service*, London, Thacker & Company, 1913, p. 418;
   The first hospital was raised on public subscription and the government provided for the medicine and equipments see Wilson, Dr. C.R., 'The First Two Hospitals in Calcutta', *Indian Medical Gazette*, Vol. 39, 1st January 1903, p. 1.
8. *Fort William India House Correspondence*, 11th April, 1785, p.?
9. *Medical Board Proceedings*, Volume January to June 1805, Letter from Colonel Green to Medical Board, June 14, 1805. p?
10. Chakrabarti, Pratick, *Materials and Medicine: Trade, Conquest and Therapeutics in the Eighteenth Century*, Manchester University Press, 2010, pp. 89-92.
11. *Report of the Committee on the Fever Hospital and Municipal Enquiry*, Vol. IV, West Bengal State Archives (WBSA) Place & year of publication, p?
12. Goode, S.M., *Municipal Calcutta, Its Institutions in their Origin and Growth*, Calcutta, Edinburgh, 1916, p. 10.
13. Clarke, John, 'Observations on the Diseases on Long Voyages to

Hot Countries and Particularly on those Which Prevail in the East Indies, 1773' cited in Harrison, Mark, *Climates and Constitution: Health, Race and British Imperialism in India 1600-1850*, OUP, 1999, p. 63. Place of publication.

14. General Department, General Branch, OC Proceedings 8 & 9, April 14, 1841, *Institution Rules and Orders Relative to Native Hospital and Dependant Dispensaries*, WBSA.
15. *Fort William India House Correspondence, 1793-95*, July 8, 1793, Consultation 137; National Archives Of India.
16. *Minutes of the Governor General Marquis of Wellesley on the Importance of Calcutta*, June 16, 1803, Report of the Fever Hospital Committee, Appendix F 301, WBSA
17. Ibid.
18. Judicial Criminal, September, 30, 1817, Consultation No-4, WBSA.
19. Strong, F.P., *On The Topography of Calcutta, the Suburbs and the Lake and the Sundarbans Beyond, 1828*, place of pub, p?
20. Jepson, Wendy, 'Of Soil, Situation and Salubrity: Medical Topography and Medical Officers in Early Nineteenth Century India', *Historical Geography*, Volume 32, 2004, p.146.
21. Martin, James Ranald, *Notes on the Medical Topography of Calcutta*, place, date of pub, p?.
22. Ibid.
23. Martin, James Ranald, op.cit, p.9.
24. Datta, Partho, op.cit, p. 19.
25. Martin, James Ranald, op.cit, p. 21.
26. *Report of the Fever Hospital Committee*, op.cit, p.
27. Muttylall Seal a wealthy businessman had donated a piece of land near Medical College for the construction of the fever hospital. See Samsad *Bangali Charitabhidhan Pratham Khanda*, place of pub, 1994, p. 391.
28. *Report of the Fever Hospital Committee*, Appendix A, op.cit,
29. Ibid.
30. Ibid.
31. Ibid.
32. Ibid.
33. Rabinow,Paul, *French Modern Norms and Forms of the Social Environment*, Massachusetts Institute of Technology, 1989, Rabinow shows that eruptive events like the cholera epidemic in 1832 in France created a new understanding of society initiating new scientific discourses, administrative concepts and marked the beginning of experiments spatial/scientific/social technology. Partho Datta feels that this is also true for Calcutta in the nineteenth century when new concepts of public health and town planning began under state initiative. Datta, Partho, op.cit, p. 26.

A History of Intimacy through Women's Self-Writings in Colonial Bengal

Aparna Bandyopadhyay

Restoring women to history and history to women is the feminist historian's modality of challenging patriarchy. From the very incipience of this discipline, history had largely been the story of men and their doings in the domain of politics, precisely, diplomacy, warfare and governance. Since women, with the exception of a few queens, princesses and rebels, had been excluded from this domain, they had remained outside the purview of history. The Marxists brought the ordinary people into history, and then the Annales school brought the nitty gritty of everyday life, emotions and sexuality into the arena of historical research.[1] The sphere of life and activity traditionally designated as private and stereotyped as the women's domain was for the first time brought within the purview of historical discussion. The genesis of women's history in the 1970s prodded by the second wave of feminism further revolutionized the discipline by exposing its androcentric bias and the politics of marginalization at work in the process of writing history. Women's history sought not just to add or insert women into history but question and challenge the very idea of history altogether. An outcome of this feminist intervention in history has been the breakdown of the dichotomy of the public and private, between the personal and the political. Feminist historians, by asserting that the personal is political, have rendered the home, the family and various aspects of domesticity as subjects of historical enquiry. Further, they have become interested in women's emotions and sexuality realizing that these are not only the sites of patriarchal control and exercise of power but also of contestation of power, the assertion of women's agency and everyday acts of resistance.

For the past two decades, I have been striving to write a history of upper caste Hindu/Brahmo women's intimate lives, especially their experiences within conjugality, their extra-marital love, and also explore the mindscapes of widows, their desires, ecstasies, agony and anguish. I wished to retrieve women's own voices in this regard. I wished to understand more adequately how women asserted their right to love and fulfilment, how they negotiated and contested in their quotidian existence the dominant ideology of a non-consensual conjugality predicated on the wife's unquestioning chastity and fidelity, how they sought to defy the patriarchal control on their minds and bodies. Women's questioning of conjugality, their love outside marriage or after widowhood, to me, epitomized the subversion of the dominant moral codes and an exercise in resistance to patriarchy. In order to understand how women interrogated and defied the dominant norms in their everyday existence and fathom the dilemmas and contrary pulls they unavoidably suffered in the process, I began to look up the autobiographies and memoirs penned by women in this period. The importance of these personal narratives and self-revelatory writings has long been recognized by feminist historians.[2] The Personal Narratives Group, for instance, in Interpreting Feminist Theory and Personal Narratives, focuses on women's personal narratives as 'essential primary documents for feminist research', including autobiographies, memoirs, diaries and letters in its list of personal narratives by women.[3]

My forays into women's life narratives in colonial Bengal were initially frustrating. Most women who had left behind autobiographies and memoirs, I found, were anxious to conform to the dominant models of womanhood, a trend also observed by Partha Chatterjee.[4] They manitained a prudish silence on their conjugal or extra-conjugal relations, their frustrations and desires, possibly to conform to the established norms of respectability. They probably did not consider it proper for women to reveal their 'deviant', defiant desires before the public eye.

Before I proceed with a discussion on women's autobiographies, it is pertinent to draw attention to the ideas of womanhood, marriage and conjugality that held sway in the mindscape of colonial Bengal.

Hegemonic Constructs of Womanhood, Marriage and Conjugality

The moral code of traditional Hindu society encompassed the norms of a woman's pre-marital chastity, of a non-elective, non-dissoluble marriage preferably contracted at the woman's infancy and predicated on the wife's monogamy and her unconditional fidelity and loyalty to husband, virtues that were expected to prevail even after the husband's death. In the ethical yardstick of that society, a woman's assertion of choice in marriage, her pre-marital intimacy, her acts of marital defiance and assertion of desire outside conjugality or in a state of widowhood were considered transgressive and severely punishable. These norms of conjugality and womanhood along with the concomitant definition of transgression were sought to be ideologically reinforced and to some extent refashioned by a section of the Bengali intelligentsia since the later decades of the nineteenth century through tracts and treatises, and also through the genre of didactic fiction labelled streepathya or satipathya (fit to be read by a woman/ chaste woman). Virtues and values imbibed from the west, thanks to exposure to western education, were considered by many historians to be integral to this process of refashioning. Partha Chatterjee has drawn attention to the conscious attempt of the Bengali intelligentsia to selectively appropriate the western virtues of orderly, aesthetic and thrifty management of the domestic space and combine these with the traditional virtues of spirituality, leading to the icon of the 'new woman'.[5] Dipesh Chakrabarty has similarly demonstrated how the synthesis of the Victorian ideal of companionate marriage and the traditional Hindu ideals of womanhood that emanated from a bid to carve out a unique modernity for the Indian nation led to the creation of the icon of the *grihalakshmi*.[6] Tapan Raychaudhuri,[7] Meredith Borthwick,[8] Judith Walsh[9] et al have drawn attention to the unprecedented importance attached to the western ideals of romantic conjugal love and the wife's roles as the enlightened companion and the help-mate of her husband, all supposedly inspired by the west. While there was undoubtedly a conscious process of appropriation of western virtues, my own readings of the available tracts and treatises reveal that the novelty of the new woman was at best cosmetic and superficial. In initial writings, especially those by Brahmo reformers, the virtues of sakhya or conjugal companionship were at times highlighted, supposedly under the influence of Victorian notions of companionate marriage,[10] with education administered within a women-specific curriculum considered a prerequisite for women to fulfil the intellectual needs of their husbands. Eventually, however, the manner in which some conjugal couples were obsessed with 'love' began to be decried. Such love was condemned as the manifestation of a spirit of individualism imbibed from western culture. That love was selfish and exclusivist as it was concentrated in the conjugal couple to the exclusion of other members of the family. That kind of love, they argued, was incompatible with the Hindu familial ethos.[11] Many writers sought to locate a different kind of love as the quintessence of conjugality. The latter kind of love, as Tanika Sarkar clearly pointed out, was superior to love of the western variety as it was not based on choice and it encompassed the entire family. It was steady, stable and everlasting.[12] Such love, especially the wife's love, it was fervently emphasized, did not precede marriage and did not die out with the husband's death. The Hindu wife was expected to embody the virtues of *satitva* and *patibratya*, virtues denoting chastity and fidelity to husband. She was supposed to love, respect her husband and be loyal to her husband irrespective of his merits or reciprocity. The ancient *gandharva*[13] and *swayamvara*[14] forms of marriage based on mutual choice were condemned as much as western style courtship. The virtues of a form of marriage based on mutual consent and limited interaction prior to marriage did not go entirely unnoticed by sections of the intelligentsia, especially by members of the Brahmo Samaj, but arranging the marriage of their wards largely remained the prerogative of guardians. In the proliferating discourses on conjugality, marriage was also portrayed as a spiritual union of souls and a harmonious fusion of body and mind with the wife deemed the man's *ardhangini*— the half-body of the husband and *sahadharmini*— co-practitioner of religious and spiritual duties. The sexual and procreative aspects of conjugality were subordinated to its more profound spiritual goals. As for *satitva* and *patibratya*, these were now subjected to threadbare analysis and redefined in emotional, intellectual and spiritual terms rather than on sexual ones and obsessively glorified as the indispensable bedrocks of conjugality. The scope of these virtues was magnified immensely beyond mere sexual fidelity to encompass a wide repertoire of responsibilities and duties to husband.[16]

A non-elective, indissoluble, love-imbued and spiritualized conjugality predicated on the wife's *satitva* and *patibratya* began to be thus obsessively harped upon by an articulate intelligentsia availing the burgeoning print culture for self-expression. While initially such a model of conjugality was upheld both by Brahmos[17] and non-Brahmo Hindus, eventually, the image of the chaste Hindu wife acquired an obsessive importance in the discourses of a revivalist Hindu nationalist intelligentsia. The conformity of women, precisely women of the upper castes, to normative codes of sexual and affective behaviour, particularly the ideals of *satitva* and *patibratya,* was emphasized by the revivalist nationalist intelligentsia as the very foundation of the spiritual supremacy of the Hindu nation.

The icon of the chaste Hindu wife, the epitome of the virtues of *satitva* and *patibratya,* and located within a non-consensual, non-dissoluble conjugality, thus emerged as the dominant archetype of womanhood since the late nineteenth century. The hegemony of this construct, however, was not beyond question. The dominant images of womanhood and conjugality were sought to be challenged and contested at various levels with alternative conceptions of marriage, womanhood and conjugality advocated, preventing the dominant construct from achieving untrammelled hegemony.[18]

Women's autobiographies and memoirs: the 'said' and the 'unsaid'

The spread of education among women since the middle of the nineteenth century enabled the emergence of the category of the *lekhika,* as aptly pointed out by Tanika Sarkar.[19] Women wrote letters and essays in newspapers and periodicals, they published manuals and monographs in the non-fictional format. They wrote novels, short stories and poems. Finally, they indulged in self-writing, penning autobiographies, memoirs and diaries.

Some Bengali women writing their selves in autobiographies and memoirs have been remarkably candid about the pre-marital courtship they had enjoyed with their would-be husbands. Instances of such candid self-revelation are Indira Devi Chaudhurani's *Smriti Samput* [A Casket of Memories],[20] Shanta Devi's *Purvasmriti* [Memories of the Past],[21] Leela Majumdar's *Pakdandi* [Winding Mountain Path],[22] Pratibha Basu's *Jivaner Jalchhabi* [Painting of Life][23] et al. These women mostly belonged to educated Brahmo/ Hindu upper caste middle class families. Their marriages had worked well, and at an advanced age, they had begun to nostalgically recount their days of pre-marital courtship, the point of entry into a successful and prosperous conjugal life. Interestingly, these accounts of pre-marital romance are thoroughly desexualized and sanitized, almost platonic. Incidentally, no Bengali *bhadramahila* writing an autobiography has recorded a failed romance. For instance, Sarala Devi Chaudhurani, it is known from other sources, had a couple of unsuccessful involvements prior to her arranged marriage with Rambhuj Dutta Chowdhury, but she writes nothing about them in her *Jivaner Jharapata* [Fallen Leaves of Life].[24]

Beena Dey, a widow who had a remarriage preceded by courtship, recounts in her memoir, Parichay [Introduction],[25] how she had met her second husband, the famous artist, Mukul Dey, and recalls her dilemmas and also the harassment she faced from various quarters in her period of courtship. Prasannamoyee Devi, a child widow with no opportunity for remarriage, briefly alludes to her 'unfulfilled desires' in her *Purvakatha* [An Account of the Past].[26] The writer, Jyotirmoyee Devi, widowed in the early twenties, was to practise austere widowhood the rest of her life. She expresses in her *Smriti-Bismritir Taranga* [Waves of Memory and Oblivion] her dilemmas and sense of guilt about exchanging letters with a male friend who had inspired her to write.[27] Apart from these brief slippages, no widow reminiscing about her early life has recorded her cravings or recounted her frustrations or her relationships in an autobiography. Finally, no married woman writing a memoir or autobiography in this period revealed her unhappiness in conjugality or any extra-marital involvement. Evidently, revealing marital disaffection or one's socially forbidden desires to the public eye was incompatible with one's 'respectability' and most women seeking to write their own life narratives could not violate this basic premise of their social existence. An exception in this regard was the doctor, Haimabati Sen.

"Because I am a woman"

Haimabati Sen's memoir, discovered and published long after her death, laid bare a horrifying saga of marital oppression, deception and exploitation in her brief conjugal life with a middle-aged deputy magistrate of Jessore, a saga that did not significantly change even after her second marriage to the Brahmo reformer Kunja Behari Sen.[28] The manuscript was unearthed by one of Haimabati's granddaughters who handed it over to Geraldine Forbes in the 1990s. Tapan Raychaudhuri translated the manuscript and the duo published the manuscript with an introduction.

Haimabati was married off at the age of twelve to a forty-five year old deputy magistrate with several children from his previous marriages. Her husband would sleep with local sex workers in their bedroom. Haimabati would tremble in fear. Her trauma led to occasional bouts of nervous collapse. Her husband's eventual death spared her more torment and moreover, prodded her to embark on a journey that culminated in her self-establishment as a doctor with a flourishing practice. In the meantime she had married a second time, this time an apparently progressive member of the Brahmo Samaj. The second marriage turned out to be even more troubled. Kunja Behari Sen was dishonest, irresponsible and abusive. He was driven out of his job on account of alleged financial irregularity. He became a mendicant for some time. He fathered several children but shirked all responsibility. He seized control over her income. Whenever Haimabati earned a few extra rupees from her professional visits she had to conceal this fact from her husband. He even beat her up from time to time. Her first husband spared her by dying, but her second husband made her life living hell. At her workplace, Haimabati refused to compromise, and protested at the slightest instance of injustice. At home, however, it is evident from her memoir, she had accepted male authority, a fact also observed by Geraldine Forbes. She became an obedient wife once she remarried. She acknowledged Kunja Behari as her master and allowed him to make crucial decisions for them both. She even bore domestic violence without much protest. The significance of Haimabati's memoir, however, lies in the fact that despite her deference to her husband, Haimabati does not try to hide the unsavoury details of her conjugal life from the public eye, nor does she try to glorify him unduly, leaving behind a manuscript which, as Forbes rightly observes, is extraordinary for its description of the burdens of a woman's life and details of marital conflict.

Autobiography in the fictional format: Na Hanyate

A woman writer at times adopted the fictional format to reveal herself. An example of this is Maitreyee Devi's Na Hanyate. (1914-1990) Na Hanyate [It Does not Die: A Romance].[29] Penned in 1974, this novel (Maitreyi Devi herself describes it as a 'novel' in the preface to the first edition of the book) is set in the backdrop of the 1930s. The names are slightly different but not entirely so—Maitreyee renamed herself Amrita, and Mircea, the man

Maitreyee was in love with, had his surname changed from Eliade to Euclid. Amrita fell in love with Mircea, a young Romanian scholar who had come to study with her father, a celebrated philosopher. The intimacy of the lovers, which extended to kisses, was discovered by Amrita's sister, Savitri, who disclosed it to their parents. Mircea was instantly expelled and made to promise that he would never meet Amrita again. A devastated Amrita came face to face with her father's hypocrisy and double standards. The latter had seemed to be very fond of Mircea but would not countenance his daughter's marriage to a foreigner. Narendranath was the archetypal patriarch who liked to hold the minds of his wife and daughters under firm leash and control their lives while he himself indulged in an extra-marital relationship. Amrita suffered terribly within and even contemplated ending her life. She eventually entered an arranged marriage with a man who demanded very little attention, and Amrita continued to hanker for Mircea within. She met Mircea much later in her life, years after Mircea wrote La *Nuit Bengali,* [Bengali Nights,][30] a sexually overloaded fictional account of their aborted courtship. While Maitreyee Devi herself admitted that she needed to write *Na Hanyate* to counter the alleged carnality of Mircea's account, this fictionalized autobiography could be re-read as a poignant representation of the vicissitudes of a woman's journey along a life that was not in her control. Here is an author revealing the inner recesses of her own mind through the voice of her fictional protagonist and articulating her anguish and trauma, denied the consummation of her love by a moral regime that did not permit a woman's marriage of one's choice, more so if it breached the cultural/racial divide. The novel is a valuable asset for a historian delving into the deviant and defiant desires of Bengali women in colonial Bengal.

Dinolipi

My queries were more satisfactorily answered once I turned my attention to diaries or *dinolipi*— as they were called in Bengali— penned by Bengali women in this period. Autobiographies represented a process of scripting of self in conformity with the expectations of the reading public. The author had in mind that the autobiography would eventually be published and therefore was hesitant about exposing her intimate inner self in writing. A *dinolipi* or diary was a form of scripting of self more candid and honest to oneself as it was not meant for a reading audience. A diary, according to Rabindranath Tagore, was a construction of self. He wrote in *Panchabhut*:

> This is one of the pitfalls of writing a diary. You have to put yourself in hesitation. One person writes a diary, another moves around in the mundane world. The diary belongs to him and he belongs to the diary.[31]

A diary, in Tagore's eyes, was a person's alter ego. Nirupama Devi, the novelist, had her reservations about a diary too. She said, 'Diary writing has its pitfalls. Diary creates an artificial life. Once it is created it tries to dominate over our real lives. A person has several levels of identity, if another artificial self is imposed on her then it becomes a problem.'[32] Tagore and Nirupama Devi had rightly understood that a diary was a form of self-construction, another form of representation of self. It might not strictly reveal what the author was actually feeling and experiencing within but then all self-revelatory writings were constructions, and in case of a diary an advantage was that the diary was not immediately intended for publication, and so the pressure to conform to societal expectations was less relentlessly at work. Writing a diary was a more spontaneous and intimate exercise, usually unstructured and unselfconscious, unmediated by an anxiety to project oneself and others in a favourable light. A diary laid bare the inner recesses of the author's psyche, the intricate layers of her subjectivity in a more poignant manner. The practice of writing a diary had started in eighteenth century Europe as a form of confession written to relieve guilt, but it was appropriated by Bengali women in the nineteenth and the early twentieth centuries to record the trivialities of their everyday existence and to release and relieve their minds.

The diaries or *dinolipi* that I have come across from this era reveal that women did not always conform to the model of unquestioning conjugality and ascetic widowhood so zealously upheld by the polemical literature of the time. Married women expressed their disaffection at the behaviour of their husbands, poured their agony and anguish at being abandoned, humiliated or abused by their husbands on the slightest pretext. Widows laid bare their inner turmoil and cravings for a special one on the pages of a diary. Thus diaries expose that women did not passively internalize the nationalist construct of womanhood, even though their autobiographies might tell a different story—a story of passive acceptance, of conformity and meticulous adherence to dominant codes of conduct.

Unhappy wives

Amiyabalar Diary is a touching chronicle of the trauma suffered by a deserted wife.[33] Amiyabala had been married at the age of sixteen to the son of an affluent aristocratic family. Her father, employed in different places in western India, had tried his best to educate his daughter and gone beyond his means to arrange her marriage to the son of an affluent, aristocratic family. For three months after her marriage, Amiyabala enjoyed conjugal bliss. Differences over dowry, however, abruptly terminated her blissful conjugality. Amiya's mother-in-law and her husband made it clear that they would not accept Amiyabala unless her father paid a sum of three thousand rupees. Amiya's father was unable to hand over the demanded amount, and Amiya was discarded forever. An exorbitant monetary demand was compounded with innumerable baseless allegations, such as these— Amiyabala was suffering from 'female disease' or 'meyeli rog', was not adequately educated, did not how to sing and play the harmonium, etc. Initially Amiyabala was optimistic that her husband would take her back but later she lost hope and sank into deep depression. She eventually died after a brief illness. Her father, unable to bear the trauma, died soon after. Amiyabala's diary was handed over to the editor of *Manasi o Marmabani* soon after her death. The editor of this periodical decided to publish fragments of this diary albeit with names changed professedly to' arouse the consciousness of society'.

Amiyabala, it appears from this diary, was deeply in love with her husband. Her love did not fade away even after he discarded her. She continued to pine for her husband and hanker for a renewed phase of conjugality. Evidently, marriage was the summum bonum of her existence. Her husband was her god, her guru, the raison d'etre of her existence. Despite being wronged and abused, she could not envisage a life away from him. She did not seek other ways of making her life meaningful. Yet she did not hesitate to criticize her husband for making a mockery of the vows of lifelong togetherness he had made at the time of their wedding. She expressed her deep sense of hurt at the injustice he had inflicted on her and criticized him for his insensitivity.

Subarnaprabha Das was the daughter of the Brahmo couple, Saradamanjari Dutta and Nabagopal Dutta.[34] Subarnaprabha was indoctrinated in Brahmoism from her childhood, and was enamoured of the Brahmo conception of conjugality as a spiritual union of souls. Betrothed to Premananda Das, son of Sundarimohan Das, another stalwart of the Brahmo Samaj, Subarnaprabha dreamt that the Brahmo ideal of conjugality would be fulfilled in her own life. After Premananda returned from America on completing higher studies, they got married. Their conjugal life, however, turned out to be a far cry from the ideal she had cherished. Subarnaprabha's diary unravels her disillusionment, her agony and anguish at Premananda's indifference, at his tendency to oppress her mentally and play the blame game on the slightest pretext. Amidst a turbulent conjugality Subarnaprobha bore several children. Evidently, there was a stark gap between precept and practice. Beneath Premananda's progressive veneer lurked a patriarchal mindset, insensitivity and double standards. His behaviour often left Subarnaprobha weeping day and night. On 13 April 1915 she wrote in her *dinolipi*:

> From morning my eyes are constantly welling up with tears. God, you know why. I lack physical and mental strength, and hence I cannot complete all the chores expected of me, and so I have to bear constant abuse. You know very well how sensitive I am, but even then if you don't understand me, then who will understand me? For you I have left my parents and come so far. I had hoped before starting the family that even if everyone else refuses to pardon me, you certainly will and from that I will get my inspiration. But now I realize that those were my dreams, unrealizable in real life ...

In her diary, Subarnaprobha complains of her weakness, but in effect she was a strong woman. She taught in a school in Shillong and was a tireless crusader for the empowerment of women. Though she could not break out of an agonizing marriage, she could not be deterred from leading a socially and politically fruitful life. Her diary unmasks the pretentiousness and double standards of men belonging to even supposedly the most progressive section of Bengali society, and also the perpetual sense of disaffection that an enlightened and sensitive woman such as Subarnaprobha harboured within marriage.

Unhappy Widows

The novelist, Nirupama Devi (1883-1951), was married at the age of ten to Nabagopal Bhatta and was widowed at the age of fourteen. She led a life of extreme austerity for the rest of her life. Her immediate post-widowhood years were spent in Bhagalpur and here she got the opportunity to interact with Saratchandra Chattopadhyay, who was yet to make a mark in the literary arena. It was here that Saratchandra reportedly fell in love with her and Nirupama's rude rebuff is known to have changed the course of Saratchandra's life. He exiled himself to Burma and while his literary career gained momentum here, eyebrows were raised about his allegedly lax and lascivious way of life. What was gossip in those times has become a fairly established fact, thanks to the personal testimony of Radharani Devi,[36] a poet close to Saratchandra, and the publication of Saratchandra's own letters, all of which testify to Saratchandra's unfulfilled love for Nirupama Devi.[37] Saratchandra and Nirupama seem to have been in touch with each other in their later years, at least through letters. Saratchandra was unhappy that Nirupama had withdrawn herself from the literary world and was becoming increasingly obsessed with rituals and worship. A conformist in her personal life, Nirupama Devi's diary, a few pages of which have been published by Chitrarekha Gupta, betrays her passion, her inner turbulence.[38]

Nirupama Devi wrote on 7 Ashar1315 (1908), 'This immense downpour of tears will drive the earth to which whirlpool of desires? God, don't let it be so. Pull me to yourself, my ocean. Pull me towards you, don't let my trivial desires prevail over you. My pacific ocean, don't be so indifferent. If you attract me towards you, this water current will not deviate elsewhere.' Evidently, Nirupama Devi was fighting within herself to suppress her desires.[39] On the same date she penned the following lines in poetry,

> On this dark night of monsoon, my mind cannot concentrate on work... my eyes are flooded with tears... why did the saint mendicant come to my doorstep? Why did he pay his veena with such pathos? Whenever I come and go my eyes fall on his face. I don't know whether to call him or rebuff him ...[40]

It is not known for certain whether Nirupama Devi reciprocated Saratchandra's feelings, but these torn pages of Nirupama's diary hint at an emotional state that was torn by contrary pulls and dilemmas. They suggest that Nirupama had to fight daily struggles within to achieve a state of equanimity.

The poet, Priyangbada Devi (1871-1935), who had lost both her husband and son early in life, developed a friendship with the Japanese artist and writer, Okakura Kakuzo, a friendship that became more and more passionate each day but was aborted by the latter's sudden and untimely death barely a year after they met. The restraint that Priyangbada exercised in her letters to Okakura[41] was strikingly missing in her notebook which records the spontaneous, uninhibited and passionate outpourings of this widow poet's yearning for Okakura.[42]

Priyangbada's notebook entries since November 1912 record the evolution of her feelings towards Okakura. Initially, all she could offer was friendship and affection. On 6th November 1912, Priyangbada Devi wrote:

> What is your need, dear friend, what would you have of me? Love, the delicate flower of a season, bearing the charm of blushing dawn, filled with nectar, pure with dew, enthralling with scent, will not bloom out of its time, and I am helpless in pain. My heart cries out against refusal and cannot let you go empty-handed. Will you then accept of me, affection? Not the product offspring of a season but the growth of a lifetime, and be my friend and foster brother for good?[43]

Love was surreptitiously and irresistibly creeping into the inner recesses of Priyangbada's existence. On 17th November 1912, she wrote:

> Why should the thoughts of a stranger scarcely known, who came into my life, just for one twilight hour, haunt me so all through the day? Does he think of me too and with hankering in his heart try to span the distant void and reach me by unceasing dreams? ...[44]

On 2nd December 1912, she wrote:

> I may not perhaps show you the fleshy bulb, but don't I reveal the soul of it in my eyes. Can't you read the poems written there through them and see the light, that never shone on any sky or sea but there?[45]

By 9th June 1913, Priyangbada was completely overpowered by a longing for Okakura. She wrote:

> Ah, why did you break my life with your longing? My past is gone, the present is quite absent, and I can build not future, try as I would. The dream-steeped, vision absorbed days are a menace to other people's routine of comfort and though I see I am wanting in consideration, I have not the strength of resistance. I glide and yield to the pressure of the intangible and leave my palpable duties undone.[46]

Okakura died on 2nd September 2013. On 11th September 2013, Priyangbada expressed herself thus:

> Was it just a year ago we met— or was it aeons before? What karma kept us apart so long, ah, what will again bring us together.[47]

On 12th September 1913, Priyangbada imagined herself in a bridal state, invested with marital insignia by her departed lover. She wrote:

> With the point of thy sharp-edged sword thou hath put the vermilion mark on my forehead— in lacquer red painted my feet, and with memory's fast iron wristlet thou hast claimed me beloved as thy bride for eternity.[48]

On 15th Sep she expressed her yearning for everlasting union by penning the following lines:

> The anniversary of our meeting of a year ago comes tomorrow - would that be the final consummation, the union everlasting ...[49]

With such passionate and soulful articulations, the romance between this young widow and the Japanese scholar comes alive on the pages of the former's notebook.

Conclusion

Diaries penned by women then are indispensable tools in the toolbox of a historian trying to write a history of intimate relations in colonial Bengal. They are more useful than autobiographies and memoirs because these were entirely meant for cathartic self-release and are supposed to be spontaneous outpourings of women's emotions. Much of what remained unsaid in autobiographies became explicit in diaries. The diaries discussed in this paper pose a serious challenge to the belief that women in colonial Bengal internalized the notions of womanhood upheld by a nationalist intelligentsia. They critiqued, contested and defied the hegemony of the ideals of *satitva* and *patibratya,* of a wife's chastity and fidelity to husband irrespective of the latter's merits and without any expectation of reciprocity, of self-effacing ascetic celibate widowhood. Wives laid bare their quest for love and understanding, the expectations they harboured within conjugality and the agony they suffered for their unfulfilled expectations, widows revealed their dilemmas, contrary pulls, their vain efforts to suppress their desires, their hankering for love and fulfillment in life. On the whole, these diaries hold the keys to the turbulent mindscapes of women in colonial Bengal, mindscapes fraught with desire, dilemma and defiance, and are thus precious to a historian seeking to create an archive of emotions in colonial Bengal.

Notes & References

1. See, for instance, Phileppe Aries and George Duby, *A History of Private Life*, Volumes 1-4, Harvard University Press, Cambridge, Massachusetts, 1987-1988;
   Theodore Zeldin, *An Intimate History of Humanity*, Harper Perennial, 1995.
2. See, for instance, Antoinette Burton, *Dwelling in the Archive, Women Writing House, Home and History in Late Colonial India*, New Delhi: Oxford University Press, 2003.
3. Personal Narratives Group, *Interpreting Women's Lives: Feminist Theory and Personal Narratives*, Indiana University Press, Bloomington and Indianapolis, 1989.
4. Partha Chatterjee, 'Women and the Nation' in *The Nation and Its Fragments: Colonial and Post-Colonial Histories*, Princeton University Press, Princeton, 1994.
5. See Chatterjee, 'The Nation and Its Women' in *The Nation and Its Fragments*, ibid.
6. Dipesh Chakrabarty, 'Difference-Deferral of (A) Colonial Modernity: Public Debates on Domesticity in British Bengal', *History Workshop Journal*, 1993.
7. Tapan Raychaudhuri, 'Love in a Colonial Climate: Marriage, Sex and Romance in Nineteenth Century Bengal' in *Perceptions, Emotions and Sensibilities: Essays on India's Colonial and Post-Colonial Experiences*, Oxford University Press, New Delhi, 1999.
8. Meredith Borthwick, *The Changing Role of Women in Bengal 1849-1905*, Princeton University Press, Princeton, 1984.
9. Judith E. Walsh, *Domesticity in Colonial India: What Women Learned when Men Gave Them Advice*, OUP, New Delhi, 2004.

10. See for instance, *Sakhidharma* [The Virtues of Companionship], *Paricharika,* Chaitra 1890. See the discussion on companionate marriage by Borthwick, *The Changing Role of Women in Bengal,* Chapter Four: Conjugal Relations, section 'The Wife as Helpmeet'. Also see Tapan Raychaudhuri, 'Love in a Colonial Climate; Marriage, Sex and Romance in Nineteenth Century Bengal', in Raychaudhuri, *Perceptions, Emotions and Sensibilities: Essays on India's Colonial and Post-Colonial Experiences*, OUP, New Delhi, 1999, p. 82.
11. See for instance *Kulabadhu Nabina o Prachina,* [The Chaste Wife: New Woman and the Old Woman], *Bamabodhini Patrika,* Falgun-Chaitra 1881 reproduced in Pradip Bose (ed.), *Samayiki: Purano Samayikpatrer Prabandha Sankalan,* vol 2; Ananda Publishers, Kolkata, 2009; *Sahadharmini,* [A Wife Associated with Husband in the Practice of Virtue], *Bamabodhini Patrika,* Pous (mid-December - mid-January) 1304 B.S. [1897-1898].
12. Tanika Sarkar, 'Hindu Conjugality and Nationalism in Nineteenth Century Bengal' in Jasodhara Bagchi (ed.), *Indian Women: Myth and Reality,* Sangam Books, Hyderabad, 1995, pp. 98-115.
    Also see Tanika Sarkar, 'Conjugality and Hindu Nationalism: Resisting Colonial Reason and the Death of a Child Wife' in *Hindu Wife Hindu Nation: Community, Religion and Cultural Nationalism,* Permanent Black, New Delhi, 2001, pp. 191-225.
13. One of the eight forms of marriage enumerated by Manu. It was based on mutual choice. The eight forms of marriage prescribed by Manu were *brahma, daiva, arsha, prajapatya, asura, gandharva, rakshasa* and *paisacha.* The first six forms of marriage could be legitimately performed by Brahmans but the first four were the ones recommended. The *asura, gandharva, rakshasa* and *paisacha* forms of marriage were sanctioned for *Kshatriyas* but only *rakshasa* was recommended for them. See *Manusamhita,* Chapter Three, shlokas 21 onwards.
14. A form of marriage where a woman chose her husband from an assembly of prospective bridegrooms, usually practised in royal families.
15. See for instance Kaliprasanna Ghose, *Bangiya Hindusamaj Sanskar* [Reform of Bengali Hindu Society], *Bangamahila,* Chaitra [mid-March - mid-April] 1875; Nagendrabala Mustafi, *Prayojoniya Prarthana* [Necessary Appeal], *Bamabodhini Patrika,* Aswin [mid-September - mid-October] 1894.
16. Nirad. C. Chaudhuri rightly points out that this obsessive glorification of *satitva* and *patibratya* was a new thing in nineteenth century Bengal. Nirad C. Chaudhuri, *Bangali Jivane Ramani* [Women in Bengali Life], Mitra o Ghosh Publishers, Calcutta, 1967.

This has also been highlighted by Sambuddha Chakravarty, *Andare Antare: Unish Shatake Bangali Bhadramahila* [The Respectable Bengali Woman in the Nineteenth Century], Stree, Calcutta, 1995, chapter on *Dampatya Bhavna* [Thoughts on Conjugality].

17. That Brahmos shared the same obsession with the ideologies of *satitva* and *patibratya* with Hindus was also observed by Arnab Saha in a recent article in *Anushtup*. In this article he also argues that a puritan sexual morality that was characteristic of a new social ethos inspired by cultural contact with the colonial west was not a pervasive ideological phenomenon. It was confined to a small section of Bengali society. See Arnab Saha, 'Byakti, Dampatya, Jounanaitiketa' [Individual, Conjugality, Sexual Morality], *Anushtup*, Pre-Autumn Number, 2008.
18. Aparna Bandyopadhyay, 'Revisiting the Women's Question in Colonial Bengal' in Aparna Bandyopadhyay and Krishna Dasgupta (eds.), *The Other Universe: An Anthology of Women's Studies*, Setu Prakashani, Kolkata, 2014.
19. Tanika Sarkar, 'Foreword' in Malini Bhattacharya and Abhijit Sen (eds.), *Talking of Power: Early Writings of Bengali Women from the Mid-Nineteenth Century to the Beginning of the Twentieth Century*, Stree, Kolkata, 2003.
20. Indira Devi Chaudhurani, *Smriti Samput* [A Casket of Memories] Vol 1, Visva-Bharati, Santiniketan, 1997 and Vol. 2, 1999.
21. Shanta Devi, *Purvasmriti* [Memories of the Past], Thema, Kolkata, 2006.
22. Leela Majumdar, *Pakdandi* [Winding Mountain Path], Ananda Publishers, Kolkata, 2007.
23. Pratibha Basu, *Jivaner Jalchhabi* [Painting of Life], Ananda Publishers, Calcutta, 1993.
24. Sarala Devi Chaudhurani, *Jivaner Jharapata* [Fallen Leaves of Life], Dey's Publishing and School of Women's Studies, Jadavpur University, Kolkata, 2007.
25. Beena Dey, 'Parichay' [Introduction], *Sharadiya Ekshan*, Calcutta, 1992, 1993 and 1994.
26. Prasannamoyee Devi, *Purvakatha* [An Account of the Past], ed. Nirmalya Acharya, Subarnarekha, Calcutta, 1982 (first published 1917).
27. Jyotirmoyee Devi, 'Smriti-Bismritir Taranga' [Waves of Memory and Oblivion], 1986, in Gourkishore Ghosh (ed.), *Jyotirmoyee Rachana Sankalan* [Collected Works of Jyotirmoyee Devi], Vol. 2, Dey's Publishing and School of Women's Studies, Calcutta, 1994.
28. Haimabati Sen, *"Because I am a woman": A Child Widow's Memoirs from Colonial India*, translated by Tapan Raychaudhuri and introduced by Geraldine Forbes, Chronicle Books, New Delhi, 2011.

29. Maitreyi Devi, *Na Hanyate* [It Does not Die: A Romance], Prima Publications, Calcutta, 1990, first published 1974.
30. Mircea Eliade, *La Nuit Bengali* [Bengali Nights], 1933.
31. Rabindranath Tagore, 'Panchabhut' [Five Elements], *Rabindra Rachanabali* [Collected Works of Rabindranath Tagore] vol. 14, Centenary Edition, Government of West Bengal, 1961, p. 629.
32. See Chitrarekha Gupta, *Nirupama Devi: Jivane o Sahitye* [Nirupama Devi: In Life and Literature], Signet Press, Kolkata, 2011, p. 194.
33. Amiyabala Devi, 'Amiyabalar Diary' [Amiyabala's Diary] in Ahana Biswas and Prasun Ghosh (eds.), *Andarer Itihas: Narir Jabanbandi* [History of the Inner Domain: Women's Testimony] vol 2, Gangchil, Kolkata, 2016.
34. Subarnaprobha Das, 'Dinolipi' [Diary], in Ishita Chakravarty, Barnali Pain and Krishna Bandyopadhyay (eds.), *Naishabdya Bhenge: Atmakathane Bharatiya Nari*, [Breaking the Silence: Self-Articulation of Indian Women] Khonj Ekhon, Kolkata, 2005.
35. Ibid, p.119.
36. Radharani Devi, 'Saratchandra: Manush o Shilpa' [Saratchandra: Man and his Art], in Abhijit Sen and Anindita Bhaduri (eds.), *Radharani Devir Rachana Sankalan* [Collected Works of Radharani Devi] vol. 2, Dey's Publishing and School of Women's Studies, Jadavpur University, 2000. First published 1976.
37. For an account of this unfulfilled relationship, See, Gopalchandra Ray, *Saratchandra*, Chapter: 'Ekti Hriday-Dourbalyer Kahini' [A Story of the Weakness of the Heart], Ananda Publishers, Kolkata, 2003.
38. Chitrarekha Gupta, *Nirupama Devi: Jivane o Sahitye*, pp. 188-195.
39. C. Gupta, op. cit., pp. 192-193.
40. Ibid, p. 193.
41. 'Letters to a Friend', *Visva Bharati Quarterly*, Autumn 1955.
42. Priyangbada Devi, *Priyangbada Devir Nirbachita Rachana: Shabda-Naishabder Chitra* [Selected Works of Priyangbada Devi: Picture of Sound and Silence], Stree, Kolkata, 1996.
43. Ibid, p. 196.
44. Ibid, p. 199.
45. Ibid, p. 205.
46. Ibid, p. 212.
47. Ibid, p. 213.
48. Ibid, p. 213.
49. Ibid, p. 214.

Reflections on History, Nation and Gender in Binodini Dasi's Autobiography: *Amar Katha*

Nirmal Bandyopadhyay

Theatre seems to have flourished in congenial environment in Bengal. 'Theatre' came to Bengal from England about two hundred years ago through the early English traders and colonial rulers of Calcutta. It was helped in its passage by two factors, firstly by the existence of an indigenous form of theatrical-friendly atmosphere in Bengal and secondly by the rise of a Bengali middle class. The emergence of this class led to the surge of interest in English dramatic literature through the spread of English education in the middle of the nineteenth century.[1] The age-old folk forms like *Jatra* in particular, as well as, *Alkap, Panchali, Putul Nach, Chhan, Gambhira, Kabigan, Kathakatha, Palagan,* and others have been popular for centuries in the vast countryside and the burgeoning townships of Bengal. Proscenuim theatre originated and developed in Calcutta which, by the end of the eighteenth century, grew into a bustling town of commerce and diverse activities, the seat of governance and the most important city of the expanding British empire in the East.

Dramatic literature forms an important part of Sanskrit, the mother of many Indian languages, including Bengali. Creative involvement with Sanskrit drama was mainly confined to the upper echelons of society and patronage for production of such plays largely to the princely courts and the aristocracy, though not exclusively so. Some sort of revival of interest in classical Sanskrit drama did take place amongst the Bengali intelligentsia in the mid-nineteenth century. It was an expression of a growing national self-consciousness, and a part of the process of deliberate quest for national pride that was consequent upon the country's conquest by England. Sanskrit plays and drama however have had minimal impact on Bengali theatre.

The immediate influence came from two sources, namely the English theatre of Calcutta and the traditional folk theatre, the *Jatra*.[2] Among the historians of Bengali theatre there is a difference in opinion as to which of the two had a dominant influence. Brajendra Nath Bandyopadhyay, a renowned scholar, is inclined to deny any link between the old Bengali *Jatra* and the Bengali theatre, a view with which many would disagree. On the other hand, Amulya Charan Vidyabhusan, another authority on the subject, upholds the opposite view that only *Jatra* can claim parentage to the Bengali theatre, a view which again is not very popular.[3] The interacting role of *Jatra*, old or new, influencing the theatre and being influenced in turn has been active throughout and continues to this day. There were others like *Jhumur, Leto, Alkap, Kathakatha, Panchali, Gambhira* etc. But *Jatra* was the most popular amongst them.

The British colonialists introduced English theatre for the entertainment of the increasing number of British administrators, traders, soldiers, and a motley crowd of heterogeneous professions who were then residing in Calcutta. It was during the energetic Governor Generalship of Warren Hastings (1772-1785) that Calcutta Theatre or the New Playhouse as it was then called was built in 1775. Others were Dum Dum Theatre, Atheneum, Sans Sauci Theatre, Chowringhee Theatre and others. The shows were at first meant exclusively for the English and the

Europeans; later, Indians were also allowed. The plays included those written by Shakespeare, Oliver Goldsmith, and many now-insignificant authors who had tremendous popularity earlier in London.

Spread of English education, growing influence of trading families, absentee landlordism, the rise of the middle class and the exploding growth of Calcutta, the strong pull of traditional Jatra among common people on the one hand and reaction against it amongst the intelligentsia, acquaintance with English dramatic literature and English theatrical forms in the playhouse of Calcutta on the other had paved the ground for Bengali theatre to grow and assume in many ways the shape it did.

By the 1830s a large and burgeoning section of affluent Bengali merchants, landholders, money lenders, rentiers, and professionals settled in Calcutta and staged shows in their palatial homes or gardens for strictly invited audience. The first such venture was noticed in 1831 and a second one in 1835. Since no original Bengali drama was available at that time, mostly translated Sanskrit classics were performed. The first original Bengali play, Ramnarayan Tarkratna's *Kulina-Kulasarbaswa* was staged in 1857. In the 1860s the emergence of a few notable dramatists partly compensated the dearth of original writing, notable among them being Michael Madhusudan Dutt and Dinabandhu Mitra who gave Bengali theatre the much-needed sustenance.

The new middle class comprising lawyers, doctors, writers, educationists, traders, the salaried people of other vocations, developed lively and many-sided interests including English drama, which they admired and aspired to imitate in their enthusiasm to have a Bengali stage. This widespread enthusiasm became articulate enough for some active amateurs and others to form an association to meet the demand. They called it the National Theatre and put up Dinabandhu Mitra's *Nildarpan* (Indigo Mirror) for the public on 7th December 1872. The response was overwhelming. The first Bengal Theatre was built and opened on 16th August 1873 wherein Michael Madhusudan Dutt's *Sharmistha* was staged. It was the first (after Lebedeff) drama ever to engage women for female roles, which men had so far played. A storm of protest erupted, as the actresses were then from the red-light area and were considered as corrupting agents. However, the protest was short-lived and other companies followed suit.

The autobiography of Binodini Dasi, *Amar Katha* (My story, 1912) is a landmark not only in the corpus of books on Bengali theatre, but also in the domain of popular women reminiscences popular in Bengal. Besides providing us with an insight into the green-room history of the Bengali stage during its formative years, it reveals Binodini's finer sensitivities in theatre, her range of understanding, and penchant in the art of acting. Girish Ghosh, her mentor in the thespian art, paid handsome tribute to her in the preface of the book.

Binodini Dasi (1863-1941) was the first celebrated actress of Bengali theatre and is considered as one of the all- time greats in the domain of theatrical art. Born in the red-light area of Calcutta, in keeping with her occupation she was apprenticed to Ganga Baiji for training in music. She first appeared on stage even before her teens in *Shatrusamhar* (Slaying the Enemy) on December 2, 1874 at the Great National Theatre. Her acting career spanned barely twelve years, ending with *Bellik Bajar* (Bazaar of the Impudent) on January 1, 1887 at Star Theatre. She performed in more than ninety roles in eighty plays on all the major theatres of her time, namely the National, Great National, Bengal and Star Theatre. She virtually sacrificed her personal resources to fund a play house which was to be named after her. But her comrades designed otherwise and christened it the 'Star Theatre', completely belying her hopes. She left theatre perhaps out of this disillusionment, severing all connections with it.

Binodini was equally proficient in serious as well as comic plays, puranic roles, and fictional ones. Her virtuosity was amazing, as six characters in one production—*Meghnad badh* (Killing of Meghnad, 1881)— and three in another in *Durgeshnandini* (... ... . daughter, 1876)— both dramatized by her mentor Girish Ghosh. The wide range of her interpretations in diverse, almost contrasting, roles testifies to her abilities. The contemporary intellectuals Bankim Chandra Chatterjee, Father Lafont, Edwin Arnold, Colonel Alcott— unanimously praised her acting. The saint Ramkrishna's arrival in the Star Theatre auditorium and the incidence of showering blessings to Binodini after watching her play *Chaitanya Lila* (Chaitanya's miracles) marked a transition for both Binodini's life and the regime of taboos and superstitions reigning supreme in social life of Bengal at that time.

One of the earliest and certainly among the most brilliant actresses of nineteenth century public theatre in Bengal, Binodini Dasi was also a powerful writer with a voice of her own. Her autobiographical writings *Amar Katha* (1912) and *Amar Abhinetri Jiban* (1924-25) along with her poems, speak of a woman who wanted much more than contemporary society was willing to grant her. Although a star in her own right and a founder member of the first actor owned theatre, Binodini was never allowed to forget her origins or her societal status.

Ever since Binodini Dasi's autobiography has seen the light of the day it has become a much valued material for social history. Binodini was also one of the many girls/ women who were being trained to perform in a novel medium, by a metropolitan intelligentsia seeking cultural identity under colonial rule. Her writings are a record of an unusually fine mind responding at multiple levels to the experiential world of the theatre. They offer unusual perspectives to evaluate and understand better the place of public theatre in the cultural history of a nation.

Binodini, in her writings, dared to articulate her fears and desires in a way that few public figures would dare to even today. On a theoretical level Partha Chatterjee discusses about women in late nineteenth century nationalist discourse. Examining the context of Bengal, Chatterjee sees a 'diminished importance of the women's question [pertaining to ... ... reform] in the period of nationalism and finds a "rather sudden disappearance of such issues from the agenda of public debate toward the close of the century".[5] He attributes this "disappearance" to middle class nationalism's location of women's "autonomous subjectivity", within the "home" instead of "the external domain of political conflict", an act through which middle-class nationalism resolved the "women's question". Partha Chatterjee argues, the history of women's struggles, then 'is to be found less in the external domain of political conflict and more in the "inner" space of the middle-class home' He amplifies his point through an analysis of "autobiographies by educated women who wrote about their lives and their struggles in this eventful period of Indian History."[6]

Rimli Bhattacharya (the translator of Binodini's autobiography, 1998) argues that Binodini's autobiography reveals middle-class nationalism's inability to accommodate the "public" woman and shows the several betrayals she faced from her teacher and guru Girish Ghosh while working in the theatre, from society, and from her patrons when she tried to build a life outside the theatre. Her analysis of Binodini's autobiography, and of "actress-stories" from early twentieth century Bengali magazines, resorts to a historicized approach that locates these texts against the backdrop of their cultural - materialist contexts.[7]

Much of the significance of Binodini's life, and indeed that of her career as an actress, arises from the fact that it coincides with the consolidation of the public theatre in Bengal. The term "public" here combines the sense of a theatre that was open to the public at large as well as that of the theatre - and indeed literature and the arts generally— as a key institution in the shaping a new civil— societal public sphere in Bengal. It was theatre, therefore, that was concerned as much with pleasure that would draw and persuade its audience, as with the intellectual, moral and aesthetic uplift of national character. The best known figures of the time were involved in the process, and clearly regarded themselves as part of a cultural vanguard, for example— Girish Ghosh, Ishwarchandra Vidyasagar, Michael Madhusudan Dutt, Swami Vivekananda.

There is another side to Binodini's autobiography. If the theatre was able to conjure a "life" for an Indian people, it was also an institution that consistently, and in many different modes, debarred the outcaste "prostitute" Binodini from that very "life". A multitude of questions arise 'because I have no relations, I am despised. I am a prostitute, a social outcast. There is no one to listen or to read what I feel within. That is why I have let you know my story in pen and papers'.[8] It is an event in which several strands in the history of modern India - genealogies of sexuality, the aesthetic, the public sphere, as also class, caste and gender— are condensed into an autobiographical moment that stages them as deception, and further, as betrayal. She wrote, 'The talented, the wise and the learned write in order to educate people, to do good to others. I have written for my own consolidation, perhaps for some unfortunate woman who taken in by deception has stumbled on to the path to hell'.[9] Binodini's scepticism grows out of reflection on her experience and involves a loss of faith in both man and god. She remarked, 'you say that if you heard the entire story of my life you would be able to explain to me how I have been created for the Lord's work. I too will unfold these incidents to you from beginning to end. If you listen you would understand how distrust has only deepened and how impossible it would be to uproot it.'[10]

Society, which had seen and appreciated males enacting the female-roles noticed sharply the shortcomings of the male enactment when they were exposed to Western literature and thoughts. This was the period when more realism was introduced in the techniques of production and which required a different form of representation. It was becoming incompatible with the ticketed staging of "theatre" and the expectations of a larger, more heterogeneous viewing public. Theatre was a financially feasible venture and the actresses were instrumental in playing their part in sustaining it. This comes across from a normal practice of the theatre companies maintaining carriages, which brought the actresses to the theatre in Calcutta.

A strong pressure had been building in Bengal to employ women to play female roles and Bengal theatre was the first which took women as actresses. Since respectable women could not be employed for acting, women from the forbidden quarters were chosen. Thus, the cultural project of the respectable domain could be fulfilled with such "loose" women. 'Actresses who were not part of the middle class cultural enterprise became instrumental in making theatre possible.'[11] The first four actresses to be recruited by a public theatre, the Bengal Theatre, were Golapsundari, Elokeshi, Jagattarini, and Shyamasundari. The National and Great National Theatres realized that they must perforce also hire actresses if only to keep up with the competition. For their play, the Great National Theatre included five actresses— Raj Kumari, Haridasi, Jadumani, Kadambini and Binodini.

The entry of the actress on stage was marked by anxiety amongst the *bhadralok* (educated class) in Calcutta because she was assumed to be a prostitute and a "public" woman who transgressed the limits of respectability. There was a strong reaction amongst the educated genteel society in Bengal, provoking a spate of letters, editorials, and speeches in public meeting.[12]

In mainstream historiography actresses, as subjects, have remained on the margins. They have also been on the fringes in subaltern and feminist historiography. Mainstream historiography find it difficult to negotiate with the actresses who unsettle many social boundaries as they do not fall in any neat category of class, caste or sexuality. In the extensive writings on theatre history and forms too, the women performers remain invisible.[13] One gets to know very little about these actresses as subjects. In its quest for giving respectability to theatre, the middle class remains uneasy in its negotiation of the social background of these actresses. But for Binodini, most of the actresses who came from poor and illiterate background, have not left behind their own accounts. Most of the evidences on them are elitist in origin. Since subalterns do not leave behind written documents, one has to work with "fragments" and "traces" to retrieve their worlds. There is a need to deconstruct the category "prostitute" actress. Binodini, in her autobiography, talks in detail about her poor background. She did not just maintain her professional status but had a strong commitment towards building theatre and furthering its cause. When Binodini's theatre company faced a crisis, she even agreed to go against her conscience for the cause of theatre to became the mistress of a wealthy businessman who was prepared to finance a new theatre only if he could have the famous Miss Binodini in exchange. Binodini was led to believe that her "brothers and sisters" in the company would express their gratitude to her by naming their new theatre after her. These very colleagues later objected to working in a theatre owned by a prostitute, and refused Binodini a share in it. The theatre family whom she trusted the most betrayed her. She felt deceived and used. Binodini talks of the duplicity of the middle class since she wanted to maintain a relationship with them but played an important role in condemning them as well. The labour and passion of the actresses was taken to fulfil the cultural needs of a middle class claiming to represent the nation but they were not given the place of respectability that the middle class had set aside for its own women.

Examining the theatre-actress's depiction in socio-political discourse in the late nineteenth and early twentieth centuries is revealing of the ways in which the politics of theatre became caught up in the nexus of social and nationalist ideologies. It resulted in the exclusion from what Benedict Anderson[14] calls the "imagined communities" of the nation. 'While artists, patrons, and managers appropriated the labour of the actress for the sustenance of urban theatre, which became a site of entertainment for a primarily middle-class audience, the politics of social class, gender, and nationalism, permeating, as they did, the theatre space, constructed the female performer/actress as the "other", of the domesticated, "pure", and "spiritual" middle class woman.[15] Hence Binodini's autobiography shows how women - as actresses have been central players in the debates on nationalism and social reform, and reveals the inevitable ways in which the public world of politics and the private worlds of women are deeply intertwined.

When actresses began performing on the stage in the late nineteenth century, their presence became a distinctly contested public issue amongst middle-class people, nationalists, and social reformers. In the mainstream, subaltern and feminist historiography, their depiction in literary texts becomes especially relevant. This is because, on one level, these texts function as cultural accounts that expose the drawbacks of theatre histories and certain kinds of autobiographical and biographical writings, which according to Nandi Bhatia[16] celebrate the highlights of the actor's artistic careers but say very little about actresses. Hence Binodini Dasi's autobiographical account is an exception.

The participation of women as actresses became a subject matter of much discussion and debate in the vernacular and English press and in the literary critical sphere. The politics of high and low culture through a discourse that places urban and folk theatre into the realm of the oppositional representation was acceptable for folk theatre to use actresses but not the urban elite theatres owned and run by the Bengal elite and duly attended by middle class spectators. Because of the unavailability of middle-class women to perform in theatres and the need to sustain theatres as financial businesses required actresses, many theatre owners opened their doors to working-class women. Yet, the simultaneous need to project theatres as 'respectable' spaces allowed them entry, provided they were reformed. That actresses also continued to be a source of irritation for some social thinkers, like, Pandit Ishwar Chandra Vidyasagar, a prominent writer and reformer, who supported and patronized the Bengal theatre but, who, upon the introduction of actresses, severed his connection with the theatre. In opposition to this view, Michael Madhusudan Dutt persuaded the theatre patrons to introduce actresses in Bengal Theatre. According to Madhusudan, 'it is very unnatural that men with signs of moustache do appear for females. If you mean theatre, you must mean actresses. Introduce women and I shall write dramas for you'.[17] It was through Madhusudan's persuasion that Bengal Theatre introduced four actresses, two of whom appeared on the opening night on stage on 16 August 1873. (According to Das Gupta [2002], the actresses were Elokashi, Jagattanini, Shyamsundari, and Golap).

The question of actresses remained central to the development of such ideas regarding theatrical activity. Women who represented the nation on public stages were accorded the task of upholding integrity of the nation. Partha Chatterjee[18] suggests, actresses posed a dual problem that concerned their position not only as public women, but also public women who were seen as belonging primarily to the rank of prostitutes. Binodini Dasi, who launched her theatre career of twelve years around this time, was the daughter of a prostitute who, suffered because of her social status despite her high stature as an actress and her contribution to the Star Theatre. Minati Chatterjee, discussing the role of actresses on the nineteenth century Bengali stage, sums up their position 'what an enigma it might have been to portray the so-called "pure" woman on stage, educate the audience in religiosity and social values in play after play, and yet remain on the margins of a nation in the making'.[19]

In this way, the respectability project of middle class was linked up with gender question. Binodini Dasi's autobiography shows how the representation of women as public performer would have undermined the respectable cultural project of middle class as female performers were stigmatized as prostitutes. To negotiate with demand for art and commerce, the middle class had no alternative in taking women from the 'loose' quarters to act in their theatres. But these women never got the social respect in their society. The social reformers in their agenda for women had remained silent on this section of women.

Besides, the actresses appear as objects and not as subjects in the middle class theatres. Inspite of their commitment to art, the whole middle class discourse on art erases the artistic traditions of women. But in theatre as a site of work, actresses' status was also that of workers and an important source of livelihood.

Hence, Rimli Bhattacharya's study on Binodini Dasi highlights how Binodini's life as a professional actress was produced by various contradictions of the new world of middle class cultural production.

Notes & Refenrences

1. Radha, Kiranmoy, *Bengali Theatre*, Delhi, NBT, 2007, p.1.
2. Ibid, p.3.
3. Ibid, p.3.
4. Chatterjee, Partha, *The Nation and its Fragments : Colonial and Postcolonial Histories*, Princeton : Princeton University Press, 1993, p. 117.
5. Ibid, p. 116.
6. Ibid, p. 137.
7. Bhattacharya, Rimli (trans. and ed.), *Binodini Dasi ; My story and My life as an Actress*, New Delhi, Kali for women, 1988.
8. Ibid.
9. Ibid, p. 107.
10. Ibid, p. 60.
11. Singh, Lata. "Foregrounding the Actresses' Question : Bengal and Maharashtra', in Singh, Lata (ed.), Play— *House of Power : Theatre in colonial India*, New Delhi, OUP, 2009, pp. 270-94.
12. Ibid, p. 276.
13. Ibid, pp. 283-84.
14. Anderson, Benedict, *Imagined Communities : Reflections on the origin and Spread of Nationalism*, London : Verso, 1983.
15. Bhatia, Nandi. *Performing Women/Reforming Womanhood : Theatre, Politics, and Dissent in North India*. New Delhi, OUP, 2010, p. XXI.
16. Ibid, p.3.
17. Dasgupta, Hemendra Nath, [1944-46]. *The Indian Stage*, 2 Vols. New Delhi : Munshiram Manoharlal Publishers, 2002, p. 229.
18. Chatterjee, Partha. op. cit.
19. Chatterjee, Minati, *Theatre Beyond the Threshold : Colonialism, Nationalism and the Bengali Stage*, New Delhi, Indialog, 2004, p. 70.

Reflection of Rural Crime and Control in Memoirs and Biography

Bidisha Chakraborty

Prior to the arrival of the British, when the Mughal controlling authority had weakened terribly, anarchy reigned in police administration. This anarchy seemed to have destroyed any system of police which ever existed. In 'Good Old Days' Carrey wrote that "The police regulations in those early days were very inefficient. Dacoits, those red-handed robbers, who ruthlessly combined most cruel atrocities with destructive pillage, abounded in many districts of Bengal, both on land and upon the rivers; and the consternation their daring exploits produced, was felt in Calcutta itself."[1] The zamindars maintained personal retainers within their zamindaris whose primary duty was collection of revenues for their masters, rather than protecting the life and property of the people. When the merchants transformed into administrators, administration of Muhammadan Law in criminal cases came into vogue that continued even after the Company established its own courts in 1772, except in matters dealt by the Regulations of 1772. The Committee of Circuit felt that since the state of the country differed from that of England, English laws were not applicable on Bengal soil. Actually, the belief that guided the Committee was that the dacoits of Bengal differed from English robbers. The Committee believed that the latter resorted to robbery driven by desperate personal wants. However, for their Indian counterpart it was a profession and sometimes even hereditary, since the families of the dacoits subsisted by the spoils they brought home. Therefore, the Committee of Circuit felt that the Indian dacoits deserved treatment as criminal wretches not fit for the leniency of English laws. Such official views are of a partisan character and therefore needs corroboration. This job of validation is possible only with the aid of non-archival or non-government sources like memoirs, autobiographies or even confessions of those criminal wretches who were blamed for creating disturbances in the countryside.

The advent of Company rule disturbed the traditional agrarian system and at the turn of the 19th century rural unrests against the new agrarian system made it imperative for the administration to establish complete government monopoly over the legitimate instruments of coercion and punishment. These instruments were also to be used to curb criminal activities in the countryside. Therefore, the creation of colonial police became a necessity.

When Lord Cornwallis arrived in 1787, the criminal courts throughout the country were in a mess. The Collectors-cum-Magistrates, busy with revenue collection (as Collectors), could wield little control over the zamindars as Magistrates. Repressive measures against banditry, robbery, murder and other criminal activities were completely ineffectual. The Governor-General-in-Council resolved to resume the superintendence of criminal justice in order to ensure a prompt and impartial administration. The Regulation of 3rd December 1790 dealt with the reform in the Fouzdari and criminal courts. Two years later, Cornwallis set himself to the task of organizing the police force for the province and the "Regulations for the police of the Collectorships of Bengal, Bihar and Orissa", considered the foundation of police Law in Bengal was passed on 7th

December 1792. It was not until the early 60s of the 19th century that a clear-cut definition of all categories of crimes was established. The Indian Penal Code of 1860 and the Police Act of 1861 were the pioneering acts in this regard.

With the decay in Mughal power, the zamindar's position underwent a change. From being mere collectors of royal rents, they gradually assumed permanent rights, which Cornwallis recognized as territorial rights. The government withdrew from active interference in the management of their estates, with some exceptions defined by law.

By the passing of the Regulation XXII of 1793 which was at first passed by Governor General Lord Cornwallis on 7th December 1792 the police establishments were redesigned throughout Bengal. The introduction of the new police system became imperative since the indigenous police system had failed to curb rural crimes. The first step taken was the removal of the rural police from the control of the zamindar. The regulation divided the country into police jurisdictions of ten coss or twenty miles square. Each division had a daroga with an establishment of armed men selected and appointed by the zilla magistrate. The daroga was to apprehend on a written charge and to take security for appearance before the Magistrate in case of bailable cases. Otherwise he was required to send the prisoners to the Magistrate within a limited time unless for petty assaults. When the parties themselves resolved to make up, the daroga could receive a written testimonial of conciliation and discharge the prisoners. This system continued till 1807 when it became expedient to make considerable alterations. The necessity for recalling zamindari aid to police assistance was envisaged because the undismissed servants of the zemindars such as the watchmen were required to cooperate with the darogas. "But a provision of this nature, without the means of prompt enforcement, has not been attended with the desired effect; ...".[2] But that did not solve the problem as pointed out by Marquis of Hastings in his Minute dated 2nd October 1815 since the Magistrates faced problems due to the lack of cordial cooperation of the zemindars. In the absence of such cooperation "... they [the Magistrates] have but little command over the village police, the officers of which necessarily look up more directly to the person who pays them than to the Government or its officers from whom they receive no wages."[3] This speaks volume about the dual nature of village police administration. Lieutenant Governor Halliday in his Minute dated 30th April 1856 mentioned the condition of the darogas. "Each of these potent functionaries was paid 25 Rupees a month, avowedly less than he could live and move about upon, and each had under him generally a Mohurer or Clerk and a Jemadar or head constable, on salaries ranging from 4 to 8 Rupees a month each, but with powers equal on most occasions to those of the Darogah himself."[4]

The Regulations of 7th December 1792 established the "thanadari system" which vested police authority, so long enjoyed by the zemindars, to government official, the daroga. The daroga or the thanadar was the head of the thannah with his entourage comprising bakshi, mohurer, jemadar, burkandaze, chowkeedar etc. Earlier referred to, the Minute dated 30th April 1856 of Lieutenant Governor Sir Fredrick Halliday it becomes obvious that the village police was an ill-paid institution where the daroga, or the head of the Thanadari system received a paltry sum of Rupees 25/- as monthly salary. However, the rural crime control system failed to function smoothly and the need for the help of the landlords or the zemindars was keenly felt. And so in the first decade of the 19th century they were again brought back to power to assist the government police officials to curb criminal activities in the countryside which was from that time onwards facing uprisings in various forms.

Despite such attempts, how far was the government successful in its mission? This paper seeks to find out whether the system of crime control by the rural police during the three decades (30s-50s) of the 19th century was flawless or was it suffering from ailment that encouraged corruption. Confessions of some dacoit prisoners and a daroga and the memoir of a daroga have been used to elicit the real rural scenario during the period under discussion.

The confessions of the dacoits primarily deal with a few points which encouraged corruption among the police officials and they also are a pointer to the role played by the rural population, both upper and lower classes. The points dealt with are:— (a) role of police; (b) role of mahajans and upper castes; (c) how individual persons were either lured or threatened to join the dacoity profession; (d) buyers of stolen goods. This paper attempts to make a brief discussion only on (a) i.e., the role of police.

In his confession, Abdul Faqueer a prisoner dacoit of Bawaleah, Zillah Rajshahye gave detailed description of the dacoities committed by him. And while doing so, he narrated the role of the darogas of thannah Rampore Bawaleah. In one such case the daroga apprended on suspicion a person named Ram Soonder, a Kait by caste. Though he was not involved in dacoity he was committed and sentenced to 7 years imprisonment. But interestingly none of the persons involved were apprehended or committed.[5] In another instance when he was asked whether the police knew about the Sardar Dacoits he replied that the daroga, mohurur and burkundazes of the thannah knew everything. And then he informed that the dacoits were apprehended by the police but on receiving remuneration in money, released them again and transmitted the case for the information of the Magistrate.[6] Again, when queried about how the Sardar Dacoits left their villages at night without the knowledge of the chowkeedars, this man replied that "All these Chowkeedars of the village are in the confederacy of the Sardars, and taking from them money, and often the Chowkeedars themselves go to commit dacoity with them."[7] Another prisoner dacoit Purshad Shenna confessed that the Sardars under whom he committed dacoities "serve as Chowkeedars, and commit dacoities."[8]

With the aid of these confessions we are able to get a glimpse of the rural world, how fear of insecurity haunted rural population. How unsafe their life was.

We find echoes of these confessions in the memoir of Daroga Girish Chandra Ghosh, in his memoir, "Sekaler Darogar Kahini" (The story of Darogas of those days) which was first published in 1888. He became a daroga in 1853 and the memoir dealt with his experiences as one. While narrating the incidents he mentioned corrupt police officials he came across in his profession. One such person was a Jemadar or head constable, about whom Ghosh used the term "ideal police personnel".[9] Ghosh described him as an "enemy of the poor and the bhadralok, but having great affection for the thieves. Though unskilled in police jobs he was knowledgeable regarding money-making...."[10] In the case in reference to which Ghosh mentioned the person, he even proposed to help Ghosh to earn money by reporting in such manner so that the criminal would be released.[11]

Ghosh's memoir also demonstrates that ex-thieves were later appointed as police officials. He writes—

"I had a burkundaze named Buddhu who was once famous for his notoriety and was a thief." He first appointed the person as a chowkeedar and then later promoted him to the post of burkundaze.[12] This confession on the part of Ghosh who was writing his memoir after more than thirty years of his appointment as a police official confirms the fact that persons appointed as Chowkeedars were themselves criminals, the fact which tallies with the confession of the dacoit prisoner Parsaud Shenna.

The other memoir, reminiscences or rather daroga Miajahn's confession, as suggested by the title of the book

"The Confessions of Miajahn, Darogah of Police, Dictated by him, translated by a Mofussilite" gives a vivid image of the rural police, the corruption that infested the system. It was published in 1867. Miajahn managed to become a daroga through the help of his brother-in-law who was in the service of the Collector. Moreover his sister was the mistress of the Collector, a fact which went in his favor. Miajahn did not receive any education but he could sign his name. And according to his brother-in-law that was enough to get the job of daroga. Being the brother of the mistress of the Collector helped him to earn more than his salary as a Chaprassi at the Collector's house. He confessed that though his salary was 4 Rupees, at the end of the month he earned approximately 20 Rupees.[13] His brother-in-law promised to make him the permanent daroga of Tezpore thannah if he acted intelligently enough in a case of dacoity and then within two years he would turn into a rich man.[14] His brother-in-law Fakeer advised him about various ways of earning money. One such source was *nazrana*. When a daroga went to investigate a dacoity in a rich person's house, he was supposed to receive *nazrana*, which was his rightful earning. Fakeer further advised him to receive this 'rightful earning' through the hand of his bakshi.[15] Besides, *nazrana* from this source the daroga received *nazranas* from the indigo planters in kind, once in a year, and from zemindars in cash during the Durga puja festival, the amount of which hovered between 20 to 100 Rupees. Average income of a daroga was approximately Rupees 1000 in a year.[16]

Throughout his confession, he reveals the corruption that prevailed in the police system. He said a daroga needed reliable persons around him to do the job of bargaining.[17] His Bakshi who received a salary of 8 Rupees, thought that the job he did was enough in return for the amount he received as salary and he did not hesitate to receive even 25 paise as bribe. Referring to his Bakshi, Miajahn commented that considering the system that prevailed in the thannas, Bakshi was quite honest in comparison to the previous daroga who did not hesitate to take bribe even from the cattle-pounds.[18] From the very first day in his job the daroga started earning. On joining his duty, the daroga met all the Chowkeedars employed under the jurisdiction of his thana. The person received 1 Rupee from each of the Chowkeedar as *nazrana*. At that time, the salary of a daroga was only 25 Rupees but on the very first day of job Miajahn managed to earn 1200 Rupees since Tezpore thanna's jurisdiction covered 1200 villages.[19] Here, he mentioned the social position or status of the Chowkeedars whose dressing style revealed that the majority hailed from families of low caste Hindus– *dom, muchi, chandal, hari* etc. Employment of Muslims as Chowkeedars was not rare and in the version of Miajahn, they were shrewd and clever. They were smart enough to give false accounts and evidences when called on the dock, whether on behalf of the daroga or the zemindar. Perjury in the court was a criterion for getting appointment as a Chowkeedar.[20]

He further confessed that even if the thanna got prior information of any riot, no action was taken since actions were not at all lucrative. Moreover, the *Chaprassis* were usually novice persons armed with sheer rusted swords.[21]

The contents of the memoir and the confessions discussed above help us to get a glimpse of rural policing in Bengal during the period under review. The system was corruption-infested. Nothing could be achieved without the payment of bribe– whether in cash or in kind. The administration, sitting in Calcutta passed acts and regulations with the intention of providing a sound administrative network throughout the Presidency that would enable the common people to get proper justice and a peaceful life. But, the village and *mofussils* administrations, far beyond the reach of the seat of power, did not act in the manner that was desired by their bosses in Calcutta.

Therefore, in the long run it was the inhabitants of the countryside who eventually suffered.

A substantial topic cannot be studied on the basis of one kind of material alone. Public records, considered to be the primary source, present the view of the government which sometimes speak nothing or little of the people. Moreover, primary source is excessively limited to the documentation of a ruling government or elite class. Here personal diaries, biographies, autobiographies or memoirs can play a vital role. The gaps existing in the public records can be filled-in through these sources. Such personal reminiscences, along with the personal life history of the author also contextualize time and space. Placing them side by side with public records, narrating and analyzing the events of the period, such personal reminiscences help us to construct history, which is not partisan. In other words, they serve to construct complete history of the time. In a sense, such personal reminiscences 'democratize' history-writing. Personal diary, autobiography or memoir of an ordinary person takes us back to the time he or she narrates and analyse. Such views may present view contrary to that of the government. But the person through his or her reminiscences shares the experiences and memories with us creating a new kind of history.

In the above discourse, we witnessed how personal reminiscences have helped us to get a glimpse of the rural police during the period under review. The confessions of the dacoit prisoners, usually hailing from low caste Hindu families (similar to the chowkeedars), in a sense also contribute as personal experiences. They serve as public and private sources at the same time. Their opinions regarding the rural official controlling authority and simultaneously their thoughts about the social controlling authority (not discussed here), being oral depositions in a sense 'democratize' history writing. The confession and memoir, written long time after retirement, of the two ex-darogas reveal the rampant corruption among the police personnel that prevailed like a malady in the society.

Thus, we may conclude that biographies, autobiographies and memoirs serve to create a new narrative of particular situations, systems, events. They not only provide us with a glimpse of the major performers in rural crime, but also help us to visualize the socio-economic condition of contemporary rural Bengal. They therefore, as oral evidences serve as important and interesting ingredients of writing history.

Notes & Refenrences

1. *Good Old Days*; Massey, p. 54 (e-book).
2. *A contribution towards a history of the Police in Bengal*; W.R. Gourlay, I.C.S.; Calcutta; 1916, p. 41.
3. Ibid.
4. *Bengal Judicial Proceedings*, June 5, 1856, Consultation No. 149.
5. *Selections from records of the Bengal Government*; p. 7.
6. Ibid, p. 18.
7. Ibid, p. 18.
8. Ibid; p. 21.
9. *Sekaler Darogar Kahini*; Girish Chandra Ghosh; Alok Ray Ashok Upadhyay (Sampadito); Calcutta; 1990, p. 43
10. Ibid, p. 43.
11. Ibid, p. 52.
12. Ibid, p. 91.
13. *Miajahn Darogar Ekrarnama;*, translation by Arindam Dasgupta; Kolkata; 2009; p. 13.
14. Ibid, p. 15.
15. Ibid, p. 21.
16. Ibid, p. 33.
17. Ibid, p. 23.
18. Ibid, p. 29.
19. Ibid, p. 30.
20. Ibid, p. 31.
21. Ibid, p. 57.

Inter-relation between History & Biography: Exploring Nineteenth Century History in Sivnath Sastri's Biographical Writing

Sumita Chakraborty

Much has been said about the identical character of writings in history, biography and memoir. But the margin of difference in all these three forms of writings hardly escapes the attention of scholars or readers, across the disciplines. Many a time history and memoir are confused with autobiography. But history narrates the events of the past independent of the life of the author. The choice of subject matter may include anything occurring in the long stretches of history ranging from past to present and the treatment of the same is expected to be undertaken in an impersonal or objective manner. Where this is not possible the sheer variety of the narrative dealing with as diverse issues as social, political, economic and cultural often render it the character of an account close to the heart of the author but far away from his personal feelings and activities of life. Thus history differs from memoir and autobiography in a significant way despite efforts to put all these three categories of writing, history, memoir and biography in the same bracket. Even the margin of difference between a memoir and an autobiography is discernible in the sense that a memoir usually differs chiefly in the degree of emphasis placed on external events, whereas writers of autobiography are concerned primarily with themselves as subject matter. A memoir talks less about the life of the author and is devoted to bring out the wholesome account of event or events by making reference to all the characters, circumstances, of a given phenomenon in which the author may or may not have any role to play. Memoirs and reminiscences thus constitute a kind of autobiographies that usually emphasize what is remembered rather than who is remembering. Here the author, instead of recounting his life deals with those experiences of his life, people and events that he considers most significant. This is best expressed by Edward Gibbon when he says "I must be conscious that no one is so well qualified as myself to describe the service of my thoughts and actions. The seventeenth English poet Abraham provides a rejoinder." It is hard and nice subject for a man to write of himself, it grates his own heart to say anything of disparagement and the readers ears to hear anything of praise from him.'

Biographies are not only personal accounts of writers keen on unfolding the ideas, activities, wisdom or philosophy of the person concerned but also provide us the necessary inputs in understanding the situation or the socio-political, cultural and economic context, the person in question is associated with. These are no less valuable than recorded histories in the sense that the hero here finds reference in the context of the situation he has actually lived during his time or has witnessed the unfolding of events bearing a direct or indirect influence on his personality. Thus, in a biography, events or incidents though appear to have developed in relation to him but actually they did not. They are indeed independent of the leading person of the biography and therefore give an idea about the dominant forces or flow of events in operation in those days. Shivnath Shastri's book *Ramtanu Lahiri O Tatkalin Banga Samaj*[1] conforms to this new genre of biographies where the author is more concerned to bring to light the forces, factors and processes of the period he was witnessed to rather than what he personally thinks or feels about them. It is a kind of interpretation in the mind of the author about the historical events that took place during his life time. But seldom does it appear to be a sketch of his own life, a portrayal of the events that revolved around him. The author was keen on protecting the sanctity of the natural flow of events with the sole purpose of unfolding the events the way they did without attempting to disrupt their historical validity even for once. Where author's own entries or interpretations were resorted to, utmost care had been taken to match them with the flow of the historical narrative so that they may not appear as aberrations to the original text.

This paper seeks to highlight the historical value of one such biography entitled Ramtanu Lahiri O Tatkalin Banga Samaj written by Sivnath Sashtri which has already earned fame as an important historical document on the affairs of the nineteenth century. The historical value of the book is attempted to be assessed under the following major heads. They are,

1. Information pertaining to some rare events of the period not available in history books.
2. Historical assessment of the forces, factors and figures believed to have played decisive roles in bringing cultural resurgence in the nineteenth century.
3. Exploding certain myths commonly in circulation in history circle.
4. Beauty of the narrative.

Sivnath Sashtri, an acclaimed writer and a social reformer of the second half of the nineteenth century here portrays a man— Ramtanu Lahiri— he was deeply associated with since his childhood and adolescent days. A noted young Bengal revolutionary Ramtanu Lahiri was one of the famous disciples of Henry Louis Vivian Derozio, the others being Dakshiranjan Mukhopadhyay, Ramgopal Ghosh,

Krishnomohan Banerjee, Taraknath Das, Rasik Krishna Mallik to name a few.[2] Written in the cultural backdrop of the Bengal Renaissance Sivnath Sashtri beautifully portrays here the forces, factors and figures who have played decisive roles in shaping up the intellectual environment as well as bringing cultural renaissance in the nineteenth century. Starting the narrative by referring to the charm of upcoming Krishnanagar city as the cultural capital of Bengal second only to Calcutta the author here has set the premise by dealing at length the renowned rajas and zamindars of Krishnanagar and the other groups of ruling elites who had lent their support in the socio-economic and cultural development of Krishnanagar over the centuries. This section also includes references to society, economy and education including other state of affairs of early colonial Bengal with absorbing details on the process of transformation from Nawabi Bengal to colonial Bengal and the cultural fascination of the rajas of Krishnanagar and their patronization of cultural events in a manner uncommon in the history of Bengal zamindars. It was this penchant for promoting cultural ambience of the region by the zamindars of Krishnanagar that, according to Sivnath Sashtri, made all the difference and had set Krishnanagar's journey to progress and prosperity unmatched in any other places of colonial Bengal.[3]

Information on some rare events not available in history books in general

In a beautiful prose style Sivnath Sashtri provides in this book a rare insight into the dominant perception and sensibilities of the age, the deteriorating moral life of people, mushrooming of Babu culture and the onset of Brahmo movement[4] under the aegis of Rammohan Roy, one of the early pioneers of the Renaissance in Bengal. The narrative on pre-colonial education system, pertaining to the structure of pathsala education in particular, with emphasis on the art of teaching, the mode of payment structure of teachers and more importantly the provisions for awarding punishments to adamant students is so endearing that it is hard to find its replication in any other historical literature of Bengal. So is the enchanting description on the different segments of the society of Krishnanagar and its different layers of social stratification which would not have been possible to narrate without a sublime sense of history. The author has no doubt excelled in narrating the social history of the nineteenth century by sheer dint of his experience, erudition and intellectual elegance. However the best part of the book seems to be the detailed description on the growth of Brahmo movement in Krishnanagar along with its associated Dharma Sabhas. The author here did not forget to take not of the fact that these developments more or less followed the popular model of development as those preceded in Calcutta. In addition to these a more informal account into David Hare's contribution to the spread of English education in Calcutta and the way he displayed his passion to reach out to students to help them in all possible ways, educational, financial and emotional– something which is not available in historical literature in general– merits special attention among many others fascinating tales in the book. These and many other such explanations on different issues endowed with a highly personalized gaze into the vision of cultural ambience of Bengal in the nineteenth century are indeed rare citations and certainly enrich our grip over the social history of Bengal Renaissance.

Short portrayal of life-histories of significant individuals of the period believed to have left their imprints on the socio-cultural resurgence of Bengal

One of the major strengths the book offers us is the short descriptions on the life and career of almost all those associated with the young Bengal movement in the nineteenth century. These accounts of leaders, who filled in the ranks of young Bengal revolutionaries, though short, are perhaps not available in any other books dealing with this period. These accounts are marvelous and are the product of not merely the knowledge of the author about them. Elaborate discussion on them by Sivnath Sastri has been possible only because he shared intimate relationship with many of them and knew them personally both as friends and also as close acquaintances. They all belonged to the same age and nourished same sentiments and indebtedness to their motherland. They were the harbingers of new ideas of reform which were being carried forward to subsequent periods by their successors. While the contribution of Ramtanu Lahiri was the main focus of discussion in the book Sivnath Sastri also brought into purview how there developed in Calcutta a particular class of neo-rich people called the Bengali Babus and how they often led degenerated life on the basis of their economic prosperity and lavish life-style. The presence of Kabiyal gan (songs) and the competition among singers, particularly between Bhola Moyra and Antony Firingi used to enthrall spectators and thousands flocked to watch such popular shows. Kabiyal songs in particular became very famous in nineteenth century Calcutta. These apart, the dirt and filth that were all around in Calcutta at that time including the poor state of drainage system and sanitation that plagued the life of people of Calcutta were also vividly portrayed by Sivnath Sastri.

In this book reference has also been made to the educational development of girls brought in by Calcutta Ladies Association, an organization of a handful of educated and enlightened ladies of Calcutta. Several girls school were reported to have come up during this period in which rich donations of some of the prominent figures like Raja Baidyanath, Raja Radhakanta Dev and Madanmohan Tarkalankar etc. merit attention. It proves that the agenda of female education was quite popular in nineteenth century Calcutta which was being supported by elite section of the society. The role of Vidyasagar in widow remarriage as well as in the spread of female education was also discussed in this context by Sivnath Sastri.[5]

Even the progress of Bengali literature in nineteenth century Calcutta including assessment of some of the literary doyens such as Madhusudan Dutta, Pyarichand Mitra, Iswarchandra Gupta, Dinabandhu Mitra and Bankimchandra chattopadhyay was also referred to by Sivnath Sastri in this book. The great transformation that Bengal literary creativity witnessed at that time did not missed the attention of Sivnath which he mentioned with equal care as he referred to the changes in other fields of his study.

In the book the exploitation of the British rule was also exposed. The British revenue experiments coincided with the advent of Bengal famine resulted in tremendous hardship for the people of Bengal. Keeping in view the plassey plunder and the consequent drainage of wealth from India and the phenomenon of de-industrialization facilitating the process of ruin of Indian handicrafts have been discussed by Sivnath Sastri in an attempt to expose the exploitative character of the colonial rule.

There is every possibility that the author has highlighted them with a specific purpose i.e., to prove a point that the contributions of the relatively second grade leaders of Bengal Renaissance namely Ramtanu Lahiri, Ramgopal Ghosh, Dakshinaranjan Mukhopadhyay, Krishnamohan Bandyopadhyay, Rasikkrishna Mallik and others were no less significant than those in the top grade, namely Rammohan, Vidyasagar, Bankimchandra Keshab and Vivekananda. Indeed the fact that many of them hailed from upper class background and were quite successful in their respective profession despite serving the cause of their motherland in ways more than one is what Sivnath Sashtri tries to underline in his book. Hence Sivnath Sashtri's take on the cultural resurgence of Bengal in the nineteenth century Bengal differs from others as he believed it to have happened in multiple layers and pockets with different genre of leaders from the top to the grassroots level at the bottom playing important roles in the phenomenon popularly called the Bengal Renaissance.[6]

Exploding certain myths commonly in circulation in history circle

In this book Sivnath Sashtri has enlightened us with some fresh inputs on historical events. According to him the idea of widow-remarriage was not actually a brainchild of Iswarchandra Vidyasagar. Long before Vidyasagar thought of working for widow re-marriage many essays had been written by the disciples of Derozio in favour of widow-remarriage and published in their journals such as *Parthenon, Inquirer* etc. In fact women's issues were popular in the agenda of all the groups of Bengal in the early nineteenth century. The Young Bengal revolutionaries, having known for their relatively radical approach, might have fought for the cause of women more aggressively than others. But their ideas hardly materialized into actions as the rebellion itself petered out within a short period after creating initial euphoria for radical reform. Sivnath Sashtri's sense of history has led him to trace the causes of moral degeneration of the middle class people in the nineteenth. While accepting the pall of gloom, chaos and confusion that was naturally to follow the process of take-over of power by the British from the hands of the Bengal nawabs, Sivnath Sashtri also felt that much of the traditional benign ethos of the Hindus had been done away with the advent of the Muhammedans as rulers. Medieval India in fact witnessed many such practices such as polygamy and polyandry, the habit of drinking liquor and keeping womenfolk under perpetual subjugation by initiating purdah system which were alien to the cultural ethos of the country.[7]

Sivnath Sastri in his book has also provided indirect reference to the emancipation of women in all respects. He believed in all-round development of women which could be only possible through imbibing secular education. In those days opinions differed as to what would be the nature of women's education. Certain conservatives like Keshab Chandra Sen and others wanted women's education to flourish along lines of religious education. They were not in favour of liberal and secular education for females. Sivnath Sastri on the other hand believed that development of women including educational development should be on equal footing as those of the males and that there should not be any discrimination between males and females on the agenda of development.[8]

These assertions, though debatable are not unhistorical. More importantly, Sivnath Sashtri has shown us categorically, more than anybody else, what all major phases of cultural or intellectual progression of the Bengal Renaissance existed and who all had contributed significantly to facilitate the process. It is no mean job to identify the major hues of cultural development of an age which was itself complex in nature and already embroiled owing to the multiplicity of voices and different ideological contestations laced with rising sentiments of anti-colonialism making their presence felt simultaneously.

Conclusion

The beauty of the narrative is that Sivnath Sashtri penned down his thoughts and feelings about the age which he belonged to and as such the credibility of the biography stands unquestioned. The narrative has thus become vivid and lucid and an iota of truth filled the heart of readers about the narrative. The problems, perspectives and progression of the age have all been referred to with equal depth. Thus the author appears to be at his best when he says in the early nineteenth century the issues that figured in the agenda of public discussion were three, namely the spread of the Brahmo movement, the introduction of English education and the Young Bengal Movement.[9] While discussing the contributions of different cultural luminaries Sivnath Sastri has also highlighted the different aspects of urban culture in nineteenth century Calcutta including its economic and cultural manifestations. He took interest in highlighting the state of education in the society particularly the spread of English education and the steps taken by the government for its promotion and propagation.

In the book Ramtanu Lahhiri O tatkalin Banga Samaj thus we find reference to the society of Bengal in all its complexities and intricacies. Almost all the affairs of the-then Bengal has found coverage in this book. The book may be characterized as representing as much of the forces, figures and complex issues of the nineteenth century as those of the ideas and perceptions of the author on them.

Notes & Refenrences

1. Sivnath Sashtri, Ramtanu Lahhiri O tatkalin Banga Samaj, (ed.) by Baridbaran Ghosh, Kolkata, New Age Publishers, 1974
2. Sivnath Sashtri, *Atmacharit*, (ed.) by Goutam Niyogi, Kolkata, Sadharan Brahmo Samaj, 1982.
3. Sivnath Sashtri, *Men I have Seen*, Kolkata, Sadharan Brahmo Samaj, 1918, p. 23.
4. Sivnath Sashtri, *The History of Brahmo Samaj*, Vol. II, Kolkata, Sadharan Brahmo Samaj, 1974, p. 86.
5. Hemlata Devi, *Pandit Sivnath Sashtri's Jibancharit*, Kolkata, Chirayat Prakashan, 2011.

6. K.L. Chattopadhyay, *Brahmo Reform Movement*, Calcutta, B.K. Pub., 1983, p. 20.
7. Sivnath Sashtri, *Ramtanu Lahhiri O tatkalin Banga Samaj*, (ed.) by Baridbaran Ghosh, Kolkata, New Age Publishers, 1974, p. 76-84.
8. Swapan Basu, *Unish Sataker Stri-siksha*, Kolkata, Bangiya Sahitya Parishad, 2014.
   Also see, Swapan Basu, *Banglar Nabachetanar Itihas*, Kolkata, Bangiya Sahitya Parishad, 1975.
9. Sivnath Sashtri, *England er Diary*, Kolkata, Bengal Publishers' Private Limited, 1948, p. 123.

Representation of Birds in the *Jahangirnama*: Narratives and Visuals

Debraj Chakraborty

Nature has always been considered as an important element for shaping human settlement pattern from remote past.[1] There has been a keen relationship between man and nature from the inception of human life. Substance and growth of society and culture to a great extent relied upon man's association and conviction to nature and judicious exploitation of natural resources.[2] Nature and its varied elements such as climate factors, forest, soil, water, flora and fauna have an important role and influence on human settlement and societies.[3] In recent past historians and social scientists have taken serious attention to understand the role of nature and its varied elements in shaping out human civilization.[4] The relationship between geographical condition, human habitats and history have been seriously explored and studied by the Annals school of historians in France, notably Lucien Febre, Marc Bloch, Fernand Braudel and E.Le Roy Ladurie.[5]

Man-nature relation in terms of environmental and ecological contexts has received impetus in course of the Renaissance in Europe during the sixteenth-seventeenth century, when new ideas, thoughts, concepts, rational thinking and scientific approaches have also been incorporated to accelerate the human society and settlement pattern.[6] In the recent past environmental history has developed as an important field of study that intends to explore different issues relating to human development pattern.[7] Writing on India's ecological past has received much attention to the scholars as an important and independent discipline as it explores nature-human relation.[8] An attempt has been made by scholars like Ramachandra Guha and David Arnold to relate environmental and ecological aspects with the different dynamism of human life and they tries to characterise the South Asian environmental history as:

> ... South Asia can be mapped out topographically by its mountain ranges and major rivers systems, by its once vast forests, its deserts, its deltas, and its offshore islands. But the region is also defined historically and culturally by its urban centres, and by the crisscrossing routes of pilgrimage and trade. It is divisible into a host of ecological zones and a score or more of linguistic and cultural regions.[9]

Ecological and geographical diversities have also been considered as major element that accelerates the process of social transformation. The practise of land use, irrigational provision, agricultural manifestation, harvesting and production process, economic substance, and overall settlement pattern largely relied upon geographical and physical state of a particular region.[10] It is interesting to note that there is a debate in Indian or South Asain context among the scholars particularly to address the question of changing settlement pattern and process of human evolution.[11] Scholars have taken zeal to manifest different ecological concerns such as climate, rainfall, river courses, natural resources, minerals, and not to miss distribution of animal life.[12] All these elements can be considered as the major regulatory for shaping out the human settlement pattern. Earlier scholars had given more attention to write on changing pattern of sate in the context of political affairs, but agriculture and irrigational aspects have dealt as a part of economic concern. But recently K. Shivarakrishnan and Ismael Vaccaro have opened up the wider prospects of the environmental history as they write:

> ... to talk of nature, is not merely to talk of entities and domains, it is always also to imagine and describe relationships and connections. It is, however, hard to capture complex relationships between human-cultural and biophysical processes quite so easily, in any instrumental language of design, action, outcome and aftermath.[13]

The scholars have taken much interest to study political, social and economic aspects of the medieval times, however, environmental concerns and wild life study has not received much attention.[14] Rather ecological past has always been considered as an adjunct part of the agrarian history of time.[15] The study of Mughal India on the basis of its natural distribution has been significantly represented in the work of Irfan Habib. His colossal work titled *An Atlas of the Mughal India* deals not only the politico-economic pattern of the Mughal era during sixteenth-seventeenth century; similarly it denotes detail information on the basis of contemporary documents regarding natural vegetation, distribution of natural resources and wild life of the country.[16] However, Habib's another master work titled *Agrarian System of Mughal India* is a major inclusion to study the geographical variation of the country with special reference to extent of cultivation, forest land, animal life, irrigational provision and many more.[17] Similarly contribution of Shireen Moosvi towards that direction is also important as her symposia paper titled *Man and Nature in Mughal Era* is considered as an important inclusion to denote the natural history and wild life of the period.[18] In recent past scholars such as Divyabhanusinh, M.A. Alvi, A. Rahman, Ashan Jan Qaisar, Raman Sukumar, Som Prakash Verma, Asok Kumar Das and Ebba Koch have contributed some writings on the theme that are reflecting the approaches of the Mughal ruler towards nature and animal life.[19] However the study of natural history under the Mughals in terms of animal life began to take shape with the writing of Salim Ali on 'Dodo'.[20] He has very minutely examined the narratives of the *Jahangirnama* and visuals of the time to study the drift of natural history under the Mughals.

Present essay is an attempt to study the pre-colonial environmental concerns in terms of animal life. Subsequently special attention has also given to study the birds as described by Jahangir in his autobiography and visual representations. Therefore, this study is broadly based on contemporary sources, miniatures and other paintings as well as travelogues to call out some untapped insights that represent notion of the state and society towards animal life, especially birds.

II

Writing on India's natural past has received impetus with the foundation of the Mughal empire in Hindustan during the early sixteenth century after the decisive first battle of Panipat (1526). The description of this land in an extensive and accurate manner appears from the contemporary chronicles.[21] Zahir ud-din Muhammad Babur (r. 1526-1530), the founder ruler of the Mughal line in Hindustan has been considered as a keen lover of nature.[22] His style of writing, analysis, observation makes him a naturalist. His autobiographical writing known as *Waqui'at-i Baburi* is one of the finest work not only in world literature, it similarly shows Babur's inquisitive mind and eagerness for the natural world. The narratives of *Baburnama* reveals his 'undiminished interest in natural history, and a singular quickness of observation and accurate commemoration of statistical details.'[23] It was originally written in Chaghatai Turki. Illustrious ruler of the Mughal line and grandson of Babur, Akbar (r.1556-1605) found the memoirs of his grandfather 'one of the most enthralling and romantic works' and he had taken interest to translate it into Persian.[24] Abdur Rahim Khan-i Khanan, a noble at the court of Akbar and well versed both in Turki and Persian was commissioned for this task. This translated text was submitted before the ruler most likely on November 24, 1589.[25] After that the artists of the Akbar's taswirkhana (imperial studio) was commissioned for making all the illustrations of the Baburnama on the basis of descriptions offered by Babur himself in great details. A new trend began to take shape with the writings of Babur which provides vivid descriptions on India's natural past on the basis of its geographical distribution.[26]

The tradition of writing on India's natural past has received considerable encouragement under Nur ud-Din Jahangir (r. 1605-27), who was a keen lover of nature. The best source of his time is *Tuzuk-i Jahangiri* or *Jahangirnama*, his autobiographical writings that reveals the natural history of the period.[27] It represents his multi-faceted personality as a sovereign padshah (Emperor) of Hindustan. Jahangir had an interest to know the nature and natural world through the process of inductive methodology of scientific inquiry that encouraged him for visual representation of the animal world through the process of experimentation, observation and the testing of hypotheses. In the early modern period Jahangir was the first ruler in South Asia who had taken scientific approaches to study the natural surroundings with his own way of understanding.[28] His close and precise observation about wild life and nature represents him as a naturalist. His autobiographical writings have been considered as an important and authentic source of information to call out many details relating to the nature and wild life of his time.[29] This text is not only a master piece on Persian literature, it is also an outstanding work that represents the natural world in a systematic manner. Representation of nature and animal life in a naturalistic manner is prevalent in the work of Jahangir. Noted ornithologist Salim Ali has rightly examined the work of Jahangir as he says:

> His Memoirs are a veritable gazetteer of natural history of India of his day, the outstanding quality of his observations and descriptions being their first-hand character and their scientific accuracy. Most of his accounts are precise enough to permit unambiguous diagnosis of the organism concerned and their value is vastly enhanced by the superb supporting illustrations which it was Jahangir's practice to get painted by Ustad Mansur or one of his school of gifted animal painters.[30]

Studying nature was an inherited quality of the Mughal rulers and this tradition got its ultimate shape at the regime of Jahangir, who was known for his love to the nature. It was Babur, the founder ruler of the Mughal line in India introduced and carried out the tradition on writing natural history of a place. The keen interest of the Mughal rulers in study of flora and fauna of the country has extended a new way of thinking.[31] Both Babur and Jahangir were interested on writing wild life, but they had common differences as it has been pointed out Jahangir himself in his autobiographical writings. He writes:

> Although King Babur has described in his Memoirs the appearance and shapes of several animals, he had never ordered the painters to make pictures of them. As these animals appeared to me to be very strange, I both described them and ordered that painters should draw them in the Jahangirnama, so that the amazement that arose from hearing of them might be increased.[32]

The visual representation of birds and some other animals was not only commissioned by Jahangir, it was his grandfather Emperor Humayun (r. 1530-40/1555-56) who had also taken interest in representing the visuals of the animal world with realistic approach and logical basis.[33] The author of Tezkereh-al Vakait, Jouher Aftabi records an incident that shows Humayun's passion for animal world and it equally represents him as an ornithologist. Jauher records it as:

> Soon after the Rana had retired the king undressed and ordered his clothes to be washed, and in the meanwhile he wore his dressing gown; while thus siting, a beautiful bird flew into the tent, the doors of which were immediately closed, and the bird caught; His Majesty then took a pair of scissors and cut some of the feathers of the animal; he then sent for a painter, and had taken a picture of the bird, and afterwards ordered it to be released.[34]

The study of natural and animal world has received more accurate performance with Jahangir as he has offered vivid descriptions of several birds and animals and that surely represent him as a keen observer of nature and birds. The study of birds was common in the Mughal lines as Babur in his memoirs has offered very realistic observations about different varieties of birds with their physical appearance, body colour, natural habitat and accurate posture.[35] Most of these birds have been painted on the basis of description that is offered by Babur in his writings.[36] Ornithological studies has received more attention in India during the pre-colonial phase with the great patronage of the Mughal rulers. Descriptions of birds and their visual representations show the keenness of the rulers for wild life and nature. The study of birds in Mughal India not only provides information about the animal alone, it also represents the landscape, natural vegetation and some other details.[37]

It is indeed Jahangir who was inspired to study nature and animal life by his illustrious great-grandfather Babur. His memoirs Tuzuk-i Jahangiri is the most delightful and authentic document of his age that records his day to day activities and personal details. This autobiographical narrative was written down by Jahangir himself till 17th regnal year, after that his learned courtier Mutamid Khan continued to writing for further few years and this work ultimately took the shape as the Tuzuk-i Jahangiri. This autobiographical text not only a first-hand account of Jahangir's years of administration, it subsequently shows his ideology and conception regarding ruling of the state.[38] The event records in the Jahangirnama at his 12 regnal year that eventually shows the necessity of the works. On that concern Jahangir writes:

> ... I ordered the clerks of my private library to make one volume of these twelve years, and to prepare a number of copies so that I might give them to my special servants, and that they might be sent to the various cities, so that administrators (arbab-i daulat) and the auspicious might adopt them as their code.[39]

The description of the Tuzuk begins from the very first day of Jahangir's accession to the throne. But it can be assumed that actual writing of history began from slightly later days of his time. The account of Jahangir has not only been considered as the simple narratives of his day to day activities, it can be rather considered as one of the finest combination of study of natural science, history and arts. The accurate observational approach that comes from the pen of Jahangir makes his autobiographical records as a naturalist of first rank. He had his own way of thinking; moreover he did not copy the tradition of Babur. His self-thought, innovative ideas, words of expression testify to the artistic quality and accurate detail of the natural history illustration created at his age.

The study of natural history under the Mughals has received serious attention during the days of Babur. The enthusiasm towards the knowledge of natural history in great detail further sharpened under the Mughals especially during the time of Akbar and then Jahangir. During the Akbari era visual representations of the natural world was immensely encouraged and it was further developed with the contribution of noted court painters like Basawan, Bhawani, Dhannu, Farrukh Chela, Kanha Lal, Anant, Tara, and not to miss the master Naqqash of the age Manohar and Mansur. The study of animal world in the Mughal India under Jahangir had been appeared as a most fascinating works as narratives and visuals both have represented with great care and accurateness.[40]

Jahangir had great interest in animal world especially in birds. In his account Jahangir has recorded different varieties of birds which were available in the different parts of the country and even some of them were exotic in nature. He made an elaborate mention of saras in his autobiographical writings. He says:

> At this time the pairing of the saras, which I had never seen before, and is reported never to have been seen by man, was witnessed by me. The saras is a creature of the crane genus, but somewhat larger. On the top of the head it has no feathers, and the skin is drawn over the bones of the head. From the back of the eye to six finger-breadths of the neck it is red. They mostly live in plains on the plains, but are occasionally seen in flocks. People bring a pair in from the fields, and keep them in their houses, and they became familiar with men. In fact, there was a pair of saras in my establishment to which I had given the names of Laila and Majnun.[41]

As a naturalist, Jahangir, like his great-grand father Babur, had immense interest in all kinds of cranes and some other water birds, resident or migratory.[42] It is notable that Jahangir had offered 'lengthy accounts of how he collected and bred saras cranes, nurtured their chicks to adulthood and recorded in detail their habits and behaviour in his autobiography which could be compared with a fieldwork of an ornithologist.'[43]

The naturalistic approach to study the animal and birds has already received encouragement in Europe by that time which also encouraged Jahangir in developing his ideas and outlook to understand the nature and natural objects with rational output. Scientists have explored the observations of the Jahangirnama on biology, botany, geology, ornithology and zoology as the finest contributions towards the study of science during his age.[44] His famous experiment of breeding saras cranes (Grus Antigone) in captivity has been recorded in his autobiographical writings and that proves his inquisitive mind with logical understanding. His vivid account on that subject also has been considered as one of the major part of the ornithological literature. Jahangir describes the mating of saras crane as:

> One day a eunuch informed me that (the) two had paired in his presence. I ordered that if they showed an inclination to pair again they should inform me. At dawn he came and told me that they were about to pair again. I immediately hastened to look on. The female having straightened its legs bent down a little: the male then lifted up one of its feet from the ground and placed it on her back, and afterwards its second foot, and, immediately seating himself on her back, paired with her. He then came down, and, stretching out his neck, put his beck to the ground, and walked once round the female. It is possible they may have an egg and produce a young one. Many strange tales of the affection of the saras for its mate have been heard. The following case has been recorded because it is very strange.[45]

There are several Mughal paintings of cranes, among which the best-known is that, a pair of cranes with the Victoria & Albert Museum, London. Noted art historian Asok Kumar Das pointed out that the painting preserved with the V& A Museum is not genuine work of Ustad Mansur.[46] Jahangir writes in his autobiography about another crane that was brought to him when he was engaged in hunting ducks on the Safapur Lake in Kashmir during his visit in the spring of 1620. He writes:

> One day, in the midst of the sport, a boatman caught and brought me a young qarqara (the demoiselle crane, Ardea virgo). It was very thin and miserable. It did not live longer than one night. The qarqara does not live in Kashmir. This had become ill and thin at the time of coming from, or going to, Hindustan, and fallen there.[47]

There is no visual representation of this bird in the Mughal studio.[48] A small image of a pair of Siberian Crane and a pair of common cranes in a composite picture of flowers in the Indo-Persian Album in the Golestan Palace Library, Tehran has been identified by eminent art historian Asok Kumar Das. In this album, different varieties of birds are liable to seen, but only the few of them such as pigeons, common cranes and Siberian cranes has been recognised.[49]

Bengal Florican (Houbaropsis bengalensis) is very common in Indian subcontinent.[50] Babur has noticed this species and recorded information in his memoirs.[51] Jahangir encountered a jar-i bur or red bustard in the pargana of Kairana near Delhi during 1619-20. He describes this incident as follows:

> On Thursday, the 27th, I halted. In these few days I was delighted with hawking the jarz (bustard or florican) and tugh-dari (also a kind of bustard). I ordered the jarz-i-bur (the red bustard?) to be weight. It came to 2¼ Jahangiri sirs, and the

> variegated (ablaq) one to 2⅛ sirs. The large tugh-dari was ¼ sir heavier than the jarz-i-bur.[52]

It is important to note that Jahangir was much fascinated by florican as he again wrote at the end of his 18th regnal year, in March 1624. He wrote about jarz or charz in more accurate manner as:

> The jarz or charz (bustard) is of two kinds: one is a mottled black and the other bur (a kind of dun colour). I now discovered that there are not two kinds, but that which is a mottled black is the male, and that which is dun-coloured is the female. The proof of it is this, that in the piebald there are testicles and in the dun one there are eggs; this has been repeatedly found on examination.[53]

Visual representation comes to us particularly with the two paintings of Jahangir's time. A painting of female Bengal Florican, which is preserved in the Indian Museum, Kolkata represents charz-i-bur in accordance with the description of Jahangir that he offered in the Tuzuk. It is drawn by Nadiru-I-Asr Ustad Mansur as in the lower border of this painting contains an inscription that shows the name of the painter. The colour composition and accurateness of this painting shows that Ustad 'Mansur was present in the entourage and made this wonderful study at the behest of the emperor' as pointed out by Asok Kumar Das.[54]

Another painting which is with the St. Petersburg Album represents male and female florican as described by Jahangir in his autobiographical writings. This painting perhaps belongs to the same age, but it does not bear the artist's signature or the autograph of the Emperor. The stylistic approach and distribution of colour in this painting clearly shows that it has been the creature of master painter Ustad Mansur.[55]

The most splendid description comes to us in connection with birds called Saj or dipper. It is extensively available in Kashmir, Murree hills, Garwal, Nepal, Sikkim, Tibet, Northern Assam, Tezpur and North East frontier areas.[56] In his autobiography, Jahangir has shown his perfect observational instinct as he represents not only the physical appearance of the bird, but also it shows the natural habitat and environs. He noticed them while on a trip to see the famous waterfall at Sukh Nag in Kashmir. He describes the bird as:

> In this stream I saw a bird like a saj. A saj is of a black colour and has white spots, while this bird is of the same colour as a bulbul with white spots, and it dives and remains for long time underneath, and then comes up from a different place. I ordered them to catch and bring two or three of these birds, that I might ascertain whether they were waterfowl and were web-footed, or had open feet like land birds. They caught two and brought them. One died immediately, and the other lived for a day. Its feet were not webbed like a duck's. I ordered Nadiru-I-Asr Ustad Mansur to draw its likeness. The Kashmiris call it gulkar, that is, "water *saj*".[57]

Presently this master painting is preserved in the Metropolitan Museum of Art. The visual representation of saj shows Mansur's accurate study of 'a group of three dippers, the mother bird sitting on a large boulder looking at a fledgling that sits with open mouth on a neighbouring rock, while another adult has dived into the fast-moving stream with only the end of its tail visible above the water. A small bittern in the lower left is about to pounce upon a fish that, anticipating imminent danger, is trying to escape.'[58]

A painting of a single bird, called 'European Goldfinch' in a hilly landscape is preserved with an unidentified album at the National Museum, New Delhi. Perhaps it is the early contribution of Ustad Mansur when he was not commissioned for the visual representation of the Baburnama. Mansur painted this bird with more care, accuracy based upon his own study.

The Goldfinch is a medium sized bird which available in open forest, woodland, orchards, gardens, and scrub in the Western Himalaya.[59]

Cheer Pheasant (Catreus wallichii) frequents in Northern India, Madhya Bharat (Central India), Bihar, Nepal, Bengal, Chhota Nagpur, Saran, Udaipur, Rajasthan and some parts of Deccan.[60] Noted ornithologist Salim Ali has shared his observation about Cher. He writes:

> ... a long-tailed West Himalayan pheasant, rather like the English hen pheasant to look at. It is buffy-white and rusty brown, barred above and mottled below with black. The long, narrow pointed 'pheasant tail', broadly barred buff and brownish black, the narrow pointed laying-down crest and the bright scarlet patch round the eyes confirm its identity ...[61]

There is no detail discussion about this bird in the writings of Jahangir. Perhaps he encountered this bird in course of his visit to Kashmir. As we are aware of this fact that many animals came to imperial court as gifts. This tradition of having animals as gifts was very much popular under the Mughals and Jahangir has recorded an account in his autobiographical writings where he shares information about qirqawul or pheasant presented to him by Basoi, the zamindar of Talwara. He writes as:

> Basoi, the zamindar of Talwara, brought me a bird, which the hill-people call jan-bahan. Its tail resembles the tail of the qirqawul (pheasant), which is also called the tazru, and its colour is exactly like that of the hen-pheasant, but it is half as large again. The circle round the eyes of this bird is red, while the orbit of the pheasant is white. The said Basoi

> stated that this bird lived in the snow-mountains, and that its food was grass and other stuff.[62]

Ustad Mansur took interest to draw a picture of this bird and he ultimately did the 'job with his usual penchant for accuracy and liveliness.'[63] Two later version copies of this unique painting are available, but the finest copy of it is in an album with the Maharaja Sawai Man Singh II Museum, Jaipur. This painting carries the signature of the artist that depicts amal-e Ustad Mansur (Work of Ustad Mansur). After examining this painting and its stylistic approach art historian Asok Kumar Das considered it as an authentic and creation of Ustad Mansur.[64]

Falconry was a favourite pastime of the Mughals and Jahangir was familiar with different types of hawks and falcons. Of all the varieties available during that time the most used falcon in falconry was the shaheen (Falco peregrinus peregrinator), "king among reports", a resident bird in India, followed by bahari (Falco peregrinus calidus), a winter visitor.[65]

The Tuzuk contains full of account of Jahangir's experiences with falcons and also recoded a detail account of specimens that he had received as gifts. Emperor Shah Abbas of Iran sent a *shunqar* with Pari Beg, the Shah's Chief Huntsman (*Mir Shikar*). The Mughals were familiar with this bird as its Central Asian origin has been identified by the scholars. Moreover, Abu'l Fazl includes this bird in his *Ain-i Akbari* in great detail.[66] Unfortunately, the falcon was mauled by a cat 'owing to the carelessness of the Mir Shikar' before it reached Jahangir's establishment. But it did not survive more than a week. *Tuzuk* reports this incident as:

> Though it was brought to Court, it did not live more than a week. What can I write of the beauty and colour of this falcon? There were many beautiful black markings on each wing, and black, and sides. As it was something out of the common, I ordered

> Ustad Mansur, who was the title of Nadiru-I-Asr (wonder of the age) to paint and preserved its likeness. I gave the Mir Shikar Rs. 2,000 and dismissed him.[67]

There are many paintings of falcons and birds with the Mughal *taswirkhana* and the task to identify the creation of Ustad Mansur is difficult one. Asok Kumar Das, in his research has identified four such paintings these are inscribed by or attributed to Ustad Mansur, while 'the number of uninscribed images runs into dozens.'[68] The most wonderful amongst these paintings is with the Maharaja Sawai Man Singh II Museum, Jaipur. This image holds an inscription, *amal-e Nadiru-I-Asr Jahangirshahi*.[69] Very surprisingly three Nagari inscriptions are found in this painting. The first one affirming it as a bahari, while second one considering it as uttam, and at the top the words Jahangir Padshah demotes its time line. Another splendid representation of falcon comes to us from the collection of the Museum of Fine Arts, Boston. This painting has been identified as finest creation of Ustad Mansur as pointed out by noted art historian Ananda Coomaraswamy.[70]

Vultures were very common in entire Indian subcontinent. It is said that Jahangir must have commissioned his mater painter Ustad Mansur for visual representation and as a result of which a 'double portrait of vulture' appears to us.[71] Stuart Carry Welch has wonderfully shared his observation about this splendid visual representation of Mansur. He writes:

> In a fire-and-brimstone palette of blacks, grays, and turkey-wattle red, Mansur arranged two incongruously elegant scavengers for the fullest aesthetic and dramatic effect. While contemplating and sketching, he noted beauty in their ugliness and understood their wise patience. Hungry-eyed, they stare like cats at goldfish, spellbound by something — perhaps enticing carrion — arranged by the artist.

> A few streaks of white and tan rocks for perching, springs of foliage, and spare brushstrokes of nim qalam (washes of earth pigments, now slightly darkened by oxidization) provide a convincingly natural stage for the macabre pair.[72]

The Mughals had great passion for rare species of birds and animals. Amongst the Mughal rulers, Jahangir had been the foremost one who took interest in exotic birds and animals as it is well documented in his memoirs.[73] In March 1612, Muqarrab Khan, a noble and esteemed courtier of Jahangir (who was also famous as a physician for treating the animals and experienced for treating elephants especially) brought a turkey cock and a monkey to the court from Goa.[74] Emperor Jahangir found that 'among these were some animals that were very strange and wonderful, such as I had never seen, and up to this time no one had known their names.'[75] Describing the turkey cock he wrote:

> One of these animals in body is larger than a peahen and smaller than a peacock. When it is in heat and displays itself, it spreads out its feathers like the peacock and dances about. Its beak and legs are like those of a cock. Its head and neck and the part under the throat are very minute of a different colour. When it is in heat it is quite red - one might say it had adorned itself with red coral - and after a while it becomes white in the same places, and looks like cotton. It sometimes looks a turquoise colour. Like a chameleon it constantly changes colour. Two pieces of flesh it has on its head look like the comb of a cock. A strange thing is this, that when it is in heat the aforesaid piece of the flesh hangs down to the length of a span from the top of its head like an elephant's trunk, and again when he raises it up it appears on its head like the horn of a rhinoceros, to the extent of two finger-breadths. Round its eyes it is always of a turquoise colour, and does not change.

> Its feathers appear to be of various colours, differing from the colours of the peacock's feathers.[76]

Jahangir himself wrote in his autobiography about the visual representation of this unique bird. A copy of this painting is available with the Victoria & Albert Museum, London which bears an inscription that read as *amal-e Bande-e dargah Nadiru-I-Asr Jahangirshahi.*[77] A copy of the turkey cock image is with the collection of the Indian Museum, Kolkata, but this image does not hold any inscription. Subsequently a copy of this painting is in the Maharaja Sawai Man Singh II Museum, Jaipur and another Turkey cock painted in Mughal India is in the Fitzwilliam Museum, Cambridge.[78]

It is important to note that Turkey cock was the native to North America. It was even unknown in Europe during the early 16th century. Cortes, was the first European who found this bird in 1518 after his conquest over Mexico. Most likely it was introduced in Europe when Cortes came back to home.[79] But in case of India, we know the date when this specious bird was introduced in the Mughal court, though the date of its first arrival in India is not known to us from the contemporary documents. Most likely it appeared in Goa in the first half of the 17th century with the Portuguese merchants, and there after it was procured by Muqarrab Khan.[80]

Another exotic bird, dodo (*Raphus cucullatus*) comes to our notice from the St. Petersburg Album at the Library of the Institute of Oriental Studies, Russian Academy of Science, St. Petersburg Branch. The stylistic approach and lively representation motif allow us to attribute it to master painter Ustad Mansur, though this painting does not holds any signature or attributory inscription. There is no textual detail or description of dodo in the *Tuzuk*. Possibly it appears after 1624 when Jahangir had stopped writing his memoirs. It can be assumed that the miniature of the dodo was most likely executed between1624 and 1627.[81] Commenting on this painting Salim Ali writes:

> The miniature, though unsigned and undated, is clearly in the unmistakable Mansur style and leaves no doubt that it is one of the series depicting strange and exotic animals that Jahangir was wont to get illustrated by his court painters immediately they came to his notice.[82]

According to Peter Mundy's description that the dodo came from the East India Company's factory at Surat where two birds brought from Mauritius sometime in 1628, almost a year after Jahangir's death.[83] The painting represents five species of birds and dodo is the central figure. Ornithologist Salim Ali shares his observation as he writes:

> The painting created something of a sensation among the gathered ornithologists since it depicted the extinct Dodo which, judging by the very lifelike presentation of the better known bird species accompanying it on the same plate, must obviously have been painted from a living model. When and where did this live dodo come from?[84]

Apart from the narratives, extensive visuals of the time represent different varieties of birds and even in many cases some of them remained unidentified and imaginary. An album of 'birds, insects and others' known as the 'Duffeuty Album' is with the Musee Guimet, Paris, contains a composition of ten birds. This painting is bearing a signature of Miskina, a master painter at the Akbar's court. This wonderful naturalistic visual had been prepared sometimes during 1595-1600. Art historian Asok Kumar Das shares his views as follows:

> The birds are carefully drawn and brightly coloured, and placed in a naturalistic landscape setting, but on closer look they appear stylized and decorative.[85]

Jahangir did not belong to the community of the scientists. But his memoirs contain a great detail on natural history and science. His meticulous understanding and observation enabled him to become a naturalist. He was indeed a great bird watcher. Every minute detail of the birds, their colour distribution, size, variety in appearance, natural habitat had been documented with such accuracy that commissioned him as an ornithologist in modern terms. In Jahangir's work not only the graphic narratives, but also the visual representation had received same importance to explore the birds of the time. The painters of his court, especially Ustad Mansur (*Nadiru-I-Asr*), has contributed a lot in the art of animal portraiture. The extensive collection of Jahangir's paintings of birds can open up some new prospective in research on natural history as well as ornithological study. The paintings which have survived the ranges of time show a number of birds which do not have any mention even in the writings of Jahangir. His memoirs mentions about the birds in a very selective ways that were with his establishment, used for hunting purpose, exotic or domesticated. But the canvas of visual representation is quite broad as it documented some rare species with great care, as we find in case of 'dodo'.

As a matter of significance one cannot ignore the contribution of Emperor Jahangir to represent nature and natural surroundings as well as animal world based on contemporary scientific thought that enabled the scientific progress of India in medieval times. Particularly his role in making ornithological study can also be considered as the most pioneering steps during his age in contemporary world history.

Notes and References

1. Romila Thapar, *From Lineage to State: Social Formations in the Mid-First Millennium B.C. in the Ganges Valley*, Oxford University Press (hereafter OUP), New Delhi, rpt. 2011, pp. 5-9;
   J.H. Steward, 'The Concept and Method of Cultural Ecology', in his *Theory of Culture Change: The Methodology of Multiliner Evolution*, University of Illinois Press, Urbana, 1955, pp. 30-42;
   Richard M. Eaton, 'Deforestation, Cultural Identity, and the Man-Nature Relationship', Special Lecture delivered at the Asiatic Society of Bangladesh, Dhaka.
   I owe my sincere thanks to my fiends Professor M. Humayun Kabir and Professor Md. Abdur Rahim of the Dhaka University for providing this article.
2. Amiya Kumar Bagchi, 'History of Human Development as the Subject of History' in his *Perilous Passage: Mankind and the Global Ascendancy of Capital*, Rowman & Littlefield Publishers, Oxford and New York, 2005, pp. 3-20;
   J.H. Steward, op. cit., pp. 30-31.
3. Ranabir Chakravarti, 'The Other Civilization: Portrayal of the Forest in Early India', in Ajit Kumar Banerjee (ed.), *Footprints in the Forest: History and Origins of Forests, Forestry and wild Life in India*, Winrock International India and Nataraj Publishers, Dehradun, 2010, pp. 93-119;
   Paul Warde, 'Energy and Natural resource Dependency in Europe, 1600-1900', in C.A. Bayly, Vijayendra Rao, Simon Szreter and Michael Woolcock (eds.), *History, historians and development policy: A necessary dialogue*, Manchester University Press, Manchester and New York, 2011, pp. 221-42.
4. Mahesh Rangarajan, 'Polity, Ecology and Landscape: New Writings on South Asia's Past', *Studies in History*, vol. 1 (1), Sage Publications, 2002, pp. 135-147;
   Ramachandra Guha, *The Unquiet Woods: Ecological Change and Peasant Resistance in the Himalaya*, (Expanded Edition), University of California Press, Berkeley, Los Angeles and London, 2000;
   Madhav Gadgil and Ramachanra Guha, *This Fissured Land: An Ecological History of India*, Oxford University Press, Delhi, 1992;
   Richard H. Grove, Vinita Damodaran and Satpal Sangwan (eds.), *Nature and The Orient*, OUP, Delhi, 1998;
   Sumit Guha, *Environment and Ethnicity in India, 1200-1991*, Cambridge University Press, Cambridge, 1999;
   Mahesh Rangarajan and K. Shivaramakrishnan (eds.), *India's Environmental History: From Ancient Times to the Colonial Period-A Reader*, Permanent Black, New Delhi, 2012;

Mahesh Rangarajan, *India's Wildlife History*, Permanent Black, New Delhi, 2001.

5. Lucien Febvre, *A Geographical Introduction to History*, (Translated by E.G. Mountford and J.H. Paxton), Routledge, London & New York, 1996;
   Marc Bloch, *French Rural History: An Essay on Its Basic Characteristics*, (Translated into English from French by Janet Sondheimer), University of California Press, Berkley & Lons Angeles, Second revised edition, 1973;
   Fernand Braudel, *The Mediterranean and the Mediterranean World in the Age of Philip II*, (Translated into English by Sain Reynolda), University of California Press, Berkley, Los Angels and London, 1995;
6. Brian W. Ogilvie, *The Science of Describing: Natural History in Renaissance Europe*, University of Chicago Press, Chicago, 2008;
   Edward Grant, *A History of Natural Philosophy from the Ancient World to the Nineteenth Century*, Cambridge University Press, Cambridge, 2007.
7. Ranjan Chakrabarti, 'Introduction', in his (ed.), *Situating Environmental History*, Manohar, Delhi, 2007, pp. 9-42;
   Mahesh Rangarajan, 'Polity, Ecology and Landscape: New Writings on South Asia's Past', in *Studies in History*, Sage Publications, New Delhi, vol. 18 (1), 2002, pp. 135-47.
8. Romila Thapar, 'Forests and Settlements' in Mahesh Rangarajan (ed.), *Environmental Issues in India: A Reader*, Pearson, Delhi, rpt. 2012, pp. 33-41;
   Romila Thapar, 'Perceiving the Forest: Early India', in Mahesh Rajgarajan and K. Shivaramakrishnan (eds.), *India's Environmental History*, pp. 105-26;
   Aloka Parasher Sen, 'Of Tribes, Hunters, and Barbarians: Forest Dwellers in the Mauryan Period', in Mahesh Rajgarajan and K. Shivaramakrishnan (eds.), *India's Environmental History*, pp. 127-51;
   Sumit Guha, 'Claims on the Commons: Political Power and Natural Resources in Precolonial India', in Mahesh Rajgarajan and K. Shivaramakrishnan (eds.), *India's Environmental History*, pp. 327-50;
   Christopher V. Hill, *Nature and Human Societies: South Asia-An Environmental History*, ABC CLIO, California, Oxford, 2008, pp. xvii-xxii.
9. David Arnold & Ramachandra Guha, 'Introduction', in David Arnold & Ramachandra Guha (eds.), *Nature, Culture, Imperialism: Essays on the Environmental History of South Asia*, OUP, New Delhi, rpt. 2005, pp. 5-6.

10. Sumit Guha, *Environment & Ethnicity in India 1200-1991*, pp. 4-6.
11. B.D. Chattopadhyaya, *Aspects of Rural Settlements and Rural Society in Early Medieval India*, K.P. Bangchi & Co., Calcutta, 1990;
    The Making of Early Medieval India, OUP, New Delhi, 1994;
    Harbans Mukhia, 'Was There Feudalism in Indian History?', *Proceedings of Indian History Congress*, 40th Session, Waltiar, 1979, pp. 229-80;
    R.S. Sharma, *Social change in Early Medieval India (c. AD 500-1200)*, People's Publishing House, Delhi, 1969.
12. Mayank Kumar, 'Introduction', in his *Monsoon Ecologies: Irrigation, Agriculture and Settlement Patterns in Rajasthan during the Pre-Colonial Period*, Manohar, Delhi, 2013, pp. 15-21.
13. K. Shivaramakrishnan and Ismeal Vaccaro, 'Introduction: Postindustrial Natures: Hyper-mobility and Place-attachments', *Social Anthropology*, vol. XIV, no. 3, 2006, pp. 301-17, especially p. 303.
14. The work of W.H. Moreland is an first serious attempt to explore the economic aspects of the Mughal India; see W.H. Moreland, *Agrarian System of Moslem India*, (First Published 1929), Low Price Publications (Henceforth LPP), Delhi rpt. 2011;
    W.H. Moreland, *India at the Dealth of Akbar: An Economic Study*, (First Published 1920), LPP, Delhi, 1995.
15. Amita Baveskar, 'Environmental History of India', in Bharati Ray (ed.) *Different Types of History*, PHISPC Series, vol. XIV, Part 4, Delhi, 2009, pp. 147-62;
    also see Ranjan Chakrabarti, 'Introduction', in Ranjan Chakrabarti (ed.), *Situating Environmental History*, Manohar Publishers,Delhi, 2007, pp. 9-42.
16. Irfan Habib, *An Atlas of the Mughal Empire: Political and Economic Maps with Detailed Notes, Bibliography and Index*, Oxford University Press (hereafter OUP), Delhi, rep. 1986.
17. Irfan Habib, *The Agrarian System of Mughal India, 1556-1707*, (Third Edition), OUP, Delhi, 2013.
18. Shireen Moosvi, 'Man and Nature in Mughal Era', Thematic Symposium on *Man and Environment in Indian History*, 54th Session, Indian History Congress (Mysore Session, 1993), Delhi, 1993, pp. 5-33.
19. Divyabhanusinh, *The End of a Trail: The Cheetah in India*, OUP, Delhi, rpt. 2002;
    'Record of Two Unique Observations of the Indian Cheetah in Tuzuk-i-Jahangiri, *Journal of Bombay Natural History Society*, vol. 84 (2), 1987, pp. 269-74; The Story of Asia's Lion, Marg, Mumbai, 2005;

M.A. Alvi and A. Rahman, *Jahangir – The Naturalist*, INSA, New Delhi, rpt. 1989;
However, the work of Ashan Jan Qaisar is not directly related to the history of natural science of the age it rather reveals some interesting insight interaction between India and Europe in the field of technology and culture and this work is important to develop an idea on India's approach to the outer world.
See, Ashan Jan Qaisar, *The Indian Response to European Technology and Culture (A.D. 1498-1707)*, OUP, Delhi, 1982;
Raman Sukumar, *The Story of Asia's Elephant*, Marg, Mumbai, 2011;
Som Prakash Verma (ed.), *Flora and Fauna in Mughal Art*, Marg, Mumbai, 2009;
Painting the Mughal Experience, OUP, Delhi, 2005;
Asok Kumar Das, *Wonders of Nature: Ustad Mansur at the Mughal Court*, Marg, Mumbai, 2012;
Mughal Painting during Jahangir's Time, The Asiatic Society Calcutta, Kolkata, 1078;
Ebba Koch, 'Jahangir as Francis Bacon's Ideal of the King as an Observer and Investigator of Nature' in *Journal of the Royal Asiatic Society*, London, Series, 3.19.3 (2009), pp. 293-338;
see the most fascinating work on bids in the Mughal painting, see S.K. Saraswati, 'Birds in Mughal Art', in *Marg*, 2(2), (1948), pp.29-41;
Zaheda Khanam, *Birds and Animals in Mughal Miniature Paintings*, D.K. Printworlds (P) Ltd., New Delhi, 2009.

20. Salim Ali, 'Dodo: A Note' in M.A. Ali & A. Rahman, *Jahangir – The Naturalist*, pp. 15-17.
21. Fuad Koprula, 'Babur-Literary Works', in *Encyclopedia of Islam*, New Edition, vol. I, pt. 2, pp. 848-85;
Mohibul Hasan, *Babur: Founder of the Mughal Empire in India*, Manohar,Delhi, 1985, pp. 192-93;
Stephen F. Dale, 'The Poetry and Autobiography of the Babur-Nama', in *Journal of Asian Studies*, 55(3), August, 1996, pp. 635-64;
Muzaffar Alam, 'The Pursuit of Persian Language: Language in Mughal Politics', in *Modern Asian Studies*, vol. 32 (2), 1998, pp. 317-49.
22. Stanley Lane-Poole, *Babar*, The Clarendon Press, Oxford, 1899, p. 12.
23. Ibid., p. 194.
24. T.C.A. Raghavan, *Attendant Lords: Bairam Khan and Abdur Rahim Courtiers & Poet in Mughal India*, Harper Collins Publishers India, Delhi, 2017,p. 260.
This work shows the poetic and literary contribution of Abdur Rahim Khan-i Khanan at the Mughal court in a very profound way;
see Asok Kumar Das, *Wonders of Nature*, p. 24-25.

25. Abul Fazl, *The Akbarnama of Abu'l Fazl*, (Translated from Original Persian Manuscripts into English by H. Beveridge), in 3 vols., B.I Series, The Asiatic Society, Kolkata rpt. 2010, vol. III, p. 862.
26. Zahiruddin Muhammad Babur, *Babur-Nama* (Memoirs of Babur), (Translated from Original Turki Text by A.S. Beveridge), in 2 vols., (Two vols. Bound in One), Low Price Publications (hereafter LPP), Delhi, rpt. 2006, pp. 480-503.
    This portion of description reveals the natural surroundings of Hindustan and its wild life and vegetation in great detail;
    see Asok Kumar Das, *Wonders of Nature*, pp. 24-25;
    see Som Prakash Verma, 'Paintings of Tuzuk-i Baburi', M.Phil Dissertation (unpublished), Aligarh Muslim University, 1971;
    M.S. Randhwa, *Paintings of the Baburnama*, National Museum, Delhi, 1983;
    Som Prakash Verma, *The Illustrated Baburnama*, Routledge, London/New York, 2016, pp. 4-33 and the chapter titled 'Description of Natural History', pp. 271-377;
    Debraj Chakraborty, 'India's Wildlife as Represented in the Baburnama: A Study' in *Modern Historical Studies: The Journal of the Department of History* (A Peer reviewed Journal), Rabindra Bharati University, Kolkata, vol. 9, (2013), pp. 98-121.
27. M.A. Ali & A. Rahman, *Jahangir – The Naturalist*, pp. 4-14;
    see Ebba Koch, 'Introduction' in *Mughal Art and Imperial Ideology: Collected Essays*, OUP, Delhi, 2001, pp. xxiii-xxvii.
28. The pioneering contribution of Jahangir to the study of Indian birds has been addressed by modern Indian ornithologist Dr Salim Ali as he writes 'His memoirs reveal him not only as a remarkably observant but also as an extraordinary rational student of birds', see his 'Ornithology in India: Its Past, Present, and Future', in Salim Ali's, *India*, (eds. A.S. Kothari and B.F. Chhapgar), OUP, Delhi, 1996, p. 19;
    also see, Ebba Koch, 'Jahangir as Francis Bacon's Ideal of the King as an Observer and Investigator of Nature', p. 297.
29. Kim Siebenhuner and Sally Church, 'Autobiographical Writings in Pre-modern Europe and Asia: A Decentred Perspective' in *The Medieval History Journal*, Sage, vol. 18 (2), (2015), pp. 193-213.
30. Salim Ali, 'Dodo: A Note' in M.A. Ali & A. Rahman, *Jahangir – The Naturalist*, p. 15.
31. In the Islamic world writing on natural history has received encouragement in the early periods also. But in pre-Mughal period there have no sufficient evidences that could provide relevant information on natural history illustration of the time. Some sixteenth-seventeenth century Deccani paintings shed some light on the study of natural history. See B. Schmitz and Z.

A. Desai, *Mughal and Persian Paintings and Illustrated Manuscripts in the Raza Library, Rampur*, Aryan Books International, Delhi, 2006, cat no. II.I.

32. Nuruddin Muhammad Jahangir, *The Tuzuk-i-Jahangiri or Memoirs of Jahangir*, (Translated by Alexander Rogers & Edited by Henrey Beveridge), in 2 vols. (Bound in One), LPP, Delhi, rpt. 1999, vol. I, p. 215;
    I have also consulted two other vols of the Jahangirnama for this research. *Jahangir, Toozuk-i-Jahangiri*, (Edited by Sir Syed Ahmad Khan), Aligarh Edition, 1863-64; *Jahangir, The Jahangirnama: Memoirs of Jahangir, Emperor of India*, (Translated, edited, and annotated by Wheeler M. Thackston), OUP, New York, 1999.
33. Som Prakash Verma, 'Paintings on Natural History', in his *Painting the Mughal Experience*, pp. 88-102.
34. Jauhar, *The Tezkereh-al Vakait or Private Memoirs of the Moghul Emperor Humayun*, (Translated into English by Major Charles Stewart), Oriental Translation Fund, London, 1832, p. 43.
35. *Babur-Nama*, pp. 493-501; in this portion Babur has offered a vivid description of the birds of Hindustan on the basis of his observation and understanding.
36. Asok Kumar Das, *Wonders of Nature*, p. 25.
37. Som Prakash Verma, *Mughal Painter of Flora and Fauna: Ustad Mansur*, Abhinav Publications, Delhi, 1999, p. 21;
    For making an understanding the approach to the animal world according to Islamic tradition see, Richard C. Foltz, *Animals in Islamic Tradition and Muslim Cultures*, One World, Oxford, 2007 (South Asian Edition), pp. 65-84.
38. Asok Kumar Das, *Mughal Painting during Jahangir's Time*, pp. 134-35.
39. *Tuzuk-i Jahangiri*, vol. II, pp. 26-27.
40. Som Prakash Verma, *Mughal Painter of Flora and Fauna: Ustad Mansur*, pp. 37-39.
41. *Tuzuk-i Jahangiri*, vol. II, p. 16.
42. *Babur-Nama*, p. 499.
43. *Tuzuk-i Jahangiri*, vol. II, pp 16, 18, 23, 25, 32, 42, 60;
    Asok Kumar Das, *Wonders of Nature*, p. 115.
44. Ebba Koch, 'Jahangir as Francis Bacon's', pp. 307-22.
45. *Tuzuk-i Jahangiri*, vol. II, pp. 16-17.
46. Asok Kumar Das, *Wonders of Nature*, p.115.
47. *Tuzuk-i Jahangiri*, vol. II, p. 176.
48. Asok Kumar Das, *Wonders of Nature*, p. 115.
49. Ibid.
50. Salim Ali, *The Book of Indian Birds*, The Bombay Natural History Society, Bombay, 1941, p. 316.

51. *Babur-Nama*, p. 498.
52. *Tuzuk-i Jahangiri*, vol. II, p. 112.
53. Ibid, vol. II, p. 292.
54. Asok Kumar Das, *Wonders of Nature*, figure V. 43, pp. 116- 18.
55. Ibid., figure V.44, pp. 117-118; for florican see Irfan Habib, *An Atlas of the Mughal Empire*, pl. 4A, 4B;
also see, M.A. Ali & A. Rahman, *Jahangir – The Naturalist*, pp. 65-66. More over florican is found mostly in Assam, East Bengal, Bihar, Oudh, Sylhet, Kumilla and chitagong in extensive number.
56. M.A. Ali & A. Rahman, *Jahangir – The Naturalist*, p. 78.
57. *Tuzuk-i Jahangiri*, vol. II, p. 157.
58. Asok Kumar Das, *Wonders of Nature*, p.112;
M.A. Ali & A. Rahman, *Jahangir – The Naturalist*, Plate XVI.
59. Asok Kumar Das, *Wonders of Nature*, p. 122.
60. M.A. Ali & A. Rahman, *Jahangir – The Naturalist*, p. 54.
61. Salim Ali, *Indian Hill Birds*, OUP, Delhi, 1949, p. 176.
62. *Tuzuk-i Jahangiri*, vol. II, p. 220; Talwara is a small town, located in the Hoshiarpur district of the present Punjab state in India.
63. Asok Kumar Das, *Wonders of Nature*, p. 122, figure V.51.
64. Ibid; Maharaja Sawai Man Singh II Museum, Jaipur, No. AG 834 (page from the Mughal Album);
Som Prakash Verma, *Mughal Painter of Flora and Fauna: Ustad Mansur*, Fig. 3;
Som Prakash Verma, *Painting the Mughal Experience*, p. 117, Fig. 16.
65. Divyabhanusinh, 'Hunting in Mughal Painting', in Som Prakash Verma (ed.), *Flora and Fauna in Mughal Art*, p. 98;
Asok Kumar Das, *Wonders of Nature*, p. 106.
66. Abul Fazl Allami, *The Ain-i Akbari*, (Translated by H. Blochmann), (3 vols bound in 2), LPP, Delhi, rpt. 2006, vol. I, pp. 304-7.
67. *Tuzuk-i Jahangiri*, vol. II, pp. 107-8.
68. Asok Kumar Das, *Wonders of Nature*, p. 106.
69. Ibid., pp. 106-7.
70. A.K. Coomaraswamy, *Catalogue of Indian Collections in the Museum of Fine Arts, Boston*, Part VI: Mughal Paintings, Harvard University Press, Cambridge, 1930,p. 51, pl. 41;
see S.P. Verma, *Painting the Mughal Experience*, p.91, Fig. 12.
71. Asok Kumar Das, *Wonders of Nature*, pp. 102-4, fig V.26;
Zaheda Khanam, *Birds and Animals in Mughal Miniature Paintings*, p. 140, fig. 68.
72. Stuart Cary Welch, Annemarie Schimmel, Marie L. Swietochowski and Wheeler M. Thackston, *The Emperors' Album: Images of Mughal India*, The Metropolitan Museum of Art, New York, 1987, p. 173, no. 45.

73. M.A. Ali, 'Jahangir's Passion for Exotic Animals', in Som Prakash Verma (ed.), *Flora and Fauna in Mughal Art*, pp. 83-93, fig. 3.
74. Ebba Koch, 'Jahangir as Francis Bacon's', pp. 298; Asok Kumar Das, *Wonders of Nature*, p. 96, fig V.19.
75. *Tuzuk-i Jahangiri*, vol. I, p. 215.
76. Ibid., vol. I, pp. 215-16.
77. Asok Kumar Das, *Wonders of Nature*, p. 96, fig. V.19.
78. http://collections.vam.ac.uk/item/O17088/painting-mansur/ (accessed on 02/04/2017).
79. Geoffrey Powell, 'Jahangir's Turkey-Cock', in *History Today*, London, vol. 20, issue 12, December, 1970, pp. 854-58; In this text Powell describes how the bird reached England from North America some decades before the Indian knew it; also see http://collections.vam.ac.uk/item/O17088/painting-mansur/ (accessed on 02/04/2017).
80. M.A. Ali & A. Rahman, *Jahangir – The Naturalist*, pp. 63-64; Plate XII.
81. Divyabhanusinh, 'A Tale of Two Animal Paintings and a Drawing', in *Marg*, vol. 54, No. 4, (2003), pp. 66-75.
82. Salim Ali, 'Dodo-A Note', in M.A. Ali & A. Rahman, *Jahangir – The Naturalist*, p. 16.
83. Peter Mundy, *The Travels of Peter Mundy, in Europe and Asia 1608-1667*, (ed. Richard Carnac Temple), vol. II (Travels in Asia 1628-1634), The Hakluyat Society, London, 1914, pp. 318-19.
84. Salim Ali, 'Dodo-A Note', in M.A. Ali & A. Rahman, *Jahangir – The Naturalist*, p. 16.
85. Asok Kumar Das, *Wonders of Nature*, p. 131, fig. V.59.

Green Regimes and Colonial Pasts : Vignettes of Botanical Garden and Histories of Marginalised People, C. 1890-1970.

Dr. Sahara Ahmed

The construction of various botanical gardens was a phenomenon of eighteenth century India. Such exemplary creations had been exalted as a scientific feat by scientists and by some environmentalists since the inception of environmentalism. It has been argued that from about the middle of the eighteenth century to about the middle of the nineteenth century the mixture of knowledge systems became more systematic in the form of emergent state environmentalism. A biographical sketch of the Botanical Garden, Kolkata, unravels certain intriguing details and tenders a piquant understanding of British attitudes. The genesis of scientific forestry and the creation of controlled landscapes endorsing commercial forestry had probable links with these 'scientific' gardens. Mono-crop cultivation and the creation of government reserves unleashed the thorny issue of displacement.

A series of legislations led to systematic abrogation of forest rights of the forest dwellers following the implementation of forest reservations. Tracing histories of the marginalised people had been facilitated by government records, legal documents, police records or revenue records.

These sources are undeniably enriching but are shorn of the accounts of the displaced. Memoirs of the marginalised illustrate nuances of their despair, vulnerability, pangs of eking out a livelihood, impressions of an alien rule and crafting alternative strategies of survival. These reminisces aid in constructing history based on memory.

This was a period in which science in the colonies is said to have been largely dependent upon and directed by metropolitan institutions.[1] Experiences of this imperial phase unravel the colonial imperatives to impose control over structures of resources. Indeed, the degree of forest depletion and subsequent agricultural expansion varied from place to place and they did differ significantly from pre-colonial to colonial regimes. The predominant nature of a commercial venture, as typified by forestry, was a characteristic feature of the colonial state.

This paper endeavours to present vignettes of the Botanical Garden Kolkata, as illustrated in a biographical work and probes into the *raison d'être* of its inception. In the process it puts forth two arguments : Firstly, the emergence of scientific forestry and rational management in late nineteenth century Bengal indicated not only the organization and formulation of knowledge in Europe, but also imposing proprietary rights on land and labour for the conquistador. In the process manipulating tree species or coveting exotic plants was integral to the forestry enterprise in India. Secondly, in wielding control over land and labour they evicted the forest dwellers and compelled them to craft alternative strategies of survival. Weaving through memoirs the second part of this paper probes into a multiplicity of forest lives trajectories and struggles in the Jalpaiguri district with the onset of colonial intervention.

The year 1886-87 being the hundredth year of the existence of the Royal Botanic Gardens, Calcutta, Dr. George King (1840-1909), who was appointed Superintendent of the same, took the opportunity of giving a sketch of the history of the Institution.[2] King eschewed the former scientific layout of the garden replacing it with an aesthetic design of carved rocks and undulating hillocks. He provided glasshouses, a conservatory and numerous pools. In 1887 he initiated the publication of the Annals of the Royal Botanical Garden, Calcutta. In 1890 with the establishment of the Botanical Survey of India he became its director.[3] His account of the Botanical Garden provides interesting insights from an insider and could invoke numerous inferences.

He succinctly narrated that the suggestion to form a Botanical Garden in Calcutta was first made to the Government in Calcutta in June 1787 by Colonel Robert Kyd, the Superintendent of the Hon'ble Company's Dockyard at Kidderpore. He was influenced by the theories of French agronomes and the physiocrats. The proposal was favourably entertained by the Governor-General, and its adoption was recommended to the Supreme Board in London during the same month, a site, of a large piece of land immediately below Colonel Kyd's private garden at Shalimar. This piece of land, besides the Botanic Garden as it is now limited, included about fifty acres, which form part of the grounds of the present Engineering College. Colonel Kyd was himself an ardent horticulturist, and he had brought together in his private garden at Shalimar a large collection of exotic plants, chiefly from the Straits. He had, therefore, all the credentials required for the post attested by King in his work.[4] Colonel Kyd remained in office till his death in 1793. On Colonel Kyd's death the Government decided to put the garden under the charge of a special officer who should have no other duty. Dr. William Roxburgh, the Company's Botanist in Madras, was therefore transferred from that Presidency and was posted at Shibpur in November, 1793.

King in his biography has expressed deep regard for the accomplishments of Dr. Roxburgh for his experiences as a botanist. He mentions that, "Dr. Roxburgh, for many years prior to his transfer, had been engaged in studying the then little known Flora of the Northern Circars in the Madras Presidency. He was a most ardent and enthusiastic botanist, and a good gardener".[5] He gives further details about his exploits as a botanist and paid tribute to the dedicated service he rendered to the institution. King elaborated that Dr. Roxburgh was the first botanist who attempted to draw up a systematic account of the plants of India. During his busy life in this country he prepared a *Flora Indica,* which contained systematic descriptions of all the indigenous plants known to him, as well of many exotics then in cultivation in the neighbourhood of Calcutta. King's biography gives certain interesting details which could be summarized as the observations of an insider. He stated that the manuscript of Roxburgh's endeavour was published posthumously, with certain interpolations by Drs. Wallich and Carey, in 1820 by his two sons, Captains James and Bruce Roxburgh, neither of whom were botanists. King eulogizes that this book was the basis of all subsequent Indian botanical works and this work justly entitled the author as the Father of Indian Botany. He enlists the contributions of Roxburgh's successors namely, Dr. Francis Buchanan (Hamilton), Dr. Nathaniel Wallich, Dr. Griffith, Dr. Falconer, Dr. Thomas Thomson, Dr. Thomas Anderson followed by Mr. C. B. Clarke. They took keen interest in the activities of the Garden simultaneously pursuing research in botany which earned them a high scientific reputation.

Richard Grove had argued that, Robert Kyd was acutely aware of the dreadful scourge of the Famine of 1770 and concentrated on the risks incumbent in famine and the extent to which a large botanical garden might avert the danger altogether. As the East India Company was reluctant to respond to such arguments, Grove submitted that Kyd "was to stress the commercial advantage that might accrue to the East India Company while significantly playing down the merits of the project for famine prevention".[6] On the contrary King's perspectives of the purpose of the Botanical Garden was succinctly stated in the following words,

> From the first foundation of the garden, it was understood that it was to be made a source of botanical information for the possessions of the Company, and at the same time a centre to which exotic plants of economic interest could be imported for experimental cultivation, and from which, in turn, they could be issued for distribution in the Company's possessions. It was also intended that it should not only be a botanical, but also a horticultural and agricultural garden. But the economic side has to by no means been neglected. At first great hopes were entertained that the spices which rendered the trade of the Company with the Moluccas and other of the Malayan Islands so valuable might be cultivated in Bengal. The earliest efforts of Colonel Kyd were, therefore, directed to the introduction of the trees which yield nutmegs, cloves and cinnamon and of the pepper vines. It was, however, speedily proved that the climate of Northern India is quite unsuited to these equatorial species ....In fact, no small part of the benefits conferred on the country by the garden in its early days was the demonstration by practical experiment that certain natural products, many of them of a most desirable kind, cannot be grown in Bengal, much money and bootless effort being thus saved to the country. The introduction of the exotic timber trees also received early attention and in the garden there still remain a few of the original mahogany trees introduced in these early years.[7]

The introduction of tea was one of the items put down in Colonel Kyd's original programme and in the final establishment of what has now become one of the most important industries in Northern India the garden bore a most important part. Potato-growing was introduced through its agency, and the cultivation of the quinine-yielding Cinchonas of the Andes was initiated and carried to a successful extent under the Superintendent of this garden. In the improvement of Indian cotton, and in the introduction both of that and of jute to the markets of Europe, the garden authorities worked cordially in collaboration with the Agri-Horticultural Society of India, quite successfully. By the introduction of some of the best kinds of sugarcane from the West Indies, and the dissemination of these to all parts of the country, a considerable improvement was effected both on the quality and quantity of the sugar crop of the country. In this matter also the Agri-Horticultural Society aided the garden authorities. Very soon after the establishment of the society, a considerable piece of land in the garden was made over to it rent-free, and on this land the Society conducted the greater part of its operations for forty years. In fact, it was not until the year 1872 that the Society's garden was transferred to its present site in Alipore. The numerous experimentations conducted produced exotic crops for commercial consumption since its inception. A few of the products were flax, hemp, tobacco, vanilla, coffee, cocoa, jalap, india-rubber, cardamoms, tapioca and cocoa from the cultivation of economic plants As regards horticulture, it may suffice to say that a large portion of the kinds of exotic plants now found in private gardens in India had been introduced to the country through the agency of this garden, and that the improved methods of cultivation adopted were to a great extent initiated here.[8]

King also mentioned certain measures taken by the authorities for the dissemination of Christian piety. In 1820 about fifty acres of land belonging to the garden were made over by Government to the Society for the propagation of Christian knowledge, and on this land the Society founded the institution previously known as Bishop's College, but since 1880 as the Government Engineering College owing to its retransfer to Government. He had also described in detail the wretched appearance of the garden when he took charge due to the ravages of a cyclone in 1867. The only trees that survived were the great banyan tree and a smaller tree of the same sort, some peepuls and country almonds, about twenty mahagony trees and some palms.

A predominantly commercial interest is evident from King's description of the activities of the Botanical Garden. Predicated on this one can argue that scientific knowledge was often manipulated by governmental designs and proclivities to cater to its priorities. Two disparate schools of opinion are identifiable : one which propagated the dessicationist approach, which linked deforestation with agriculture, health and climate and the other was the primacy given to commercial interest or revenue enhancement measures of the colonial government. The latter school's opinion overwhelmed the concerns of the former, which still seemed to be in its nascent form. For instance, Roxburgh spent much of his time as a surgeon in Nagore and in supervising the construction of an acclimatization and botanical garden at Sammulcottah, north of Madras. Ultimately, the experiences of famines increased his interest in planting trees both to provide famine foods and try to increase the incidence of rainfall.[9] Nathaniel Wallich severely criticized the measure by which the bamboo jungle in Bengal had been cut down by government as it was supposed to be the cause of local epidemics in 1815-16. Hence these sporadic efforts received accolades from King, "Botanically the most important feature in the garden is its Herbarium, or collection of dried plants which have been distributed by Wallich to scientific institutions abroad".[10] The account further substantiates that it consisted of plants contributed by almost every worker at Botany in India since Nathaniel Wallich's return in 1832. Interchanges had taken place with other European Botanic Institutions, such as the Herbarium of the British Museum, of the Jardin des Plantes, Paris, the Imperial Gardens at St. Petersburgh and Berlin. The report lauded the contributions of Dr. King, whose skill, taste and assiduity were fully recognized by Sir Ashley Eden and supported by him with liberal grants of money and the garden was even eulogized as the best of its kind in Asia.[11] Hence a group of foresters assumed the mantle of scientific expertise and became integral to forestry operations by the end of the nineteenth century.

Vignettes of this biography was a precursor to the forestry enterprise reminiscent of a premeditated policy on forestry and the significance ascribed to science and environment as understood in the nineteenth century by the colonial government. The implementation of the colonial forest policy after the promulgation of the Government Forest Act of 1865 was a history of unparalleled destruction of forests but also heralded the demarcation of forestland for creation of reserves to facilitate monocrop cultivation.

II

In this attempt to control man and forest the marginalization of the forest dweller became inevitable. In this part of the paper by focusing on memoirs (based on fieldwork and narrative accounts) I shall try to construct a multiplicity of forest lives trajectories and struggles in the Jalpaiguri district with the onset of colonial intervention.

The population of the district was not a homogenous one. Jalpaiguri was the homeland of several autochthonous groups : Meches, Garos, Rabhas and Totos. There was a large colony of the Meches on the borders of Nepal and India along the river Mechi. The Totos resided on the eastern bank of the river Teesta and its confluence of the river Leesh. The Rabhas lived in the forest of the north-eastern part of West Bengal. Prior to colonial intervention the Western Duars part of Jalpaiguri was under Bhutanese subjugation.

B.G. Karlsson's seminal work on the Rabhas narrates the following account given by a Rabha man (60 years old), who claimed he heard it from his grandfather, is an instance of the most commonly retold themes:

> Formerly the Bhutanese Raja ruled here. He came riding on a horse and collected taxes from Kochas. If people could not pay the kajan of three rupees (for each household), the Raja stayed in the village until the women could supply an equivalent amount of cloth. The women had to serve meat, chicken and jau (rice-beer) to the Raja. The Bhutanese kingdom then reached all the way to Cooch Behar. But later the British and Bhutanese started a war against each other. The British company made a camp along the Torsa River. They needed drinking water. The Bhutanese found out that they were taking water from the river daily, so they poisoned the water with a toxic fruit. The British commandant died and was buried at a place called *Sahib potta* (sahib grave). After this the British army was about to disintegrate, but one of the captains, named Ali babu, managed to reorganize the army, and finally led his troops to a victory over the Bhutias. The battle took place beside the Torsa River, close to the present town of Hasimara. Ali babu then invited all the Rajas in the area to big feast. The place where the feast was held is today called Rajabathkawa which means "where the Rajas had rice". After this, the Kochas were told by the British that they no longer could move about and clear new land in the forest. They now had to settle down in one place. The British also said that black people from the south are coming, and there would be no room for us to move around. The forest was divided, and we had to come to special areas chosen for us. These are the same places where we now live.[12]

One can infer that the Bhutanese raja regularly collected taxes from them and those who failed to pay were penalized.

The Anglo-Bhutanese War had subjugated the Bhutanese but the Kochas had to submit to the British who restricted their frequent change of residence for shifting cultivation due to the reservation of forests. They confronted a further displacement with the immigration of Santhals, Oraons and others from the Chotanagpur region referred to as the 'black people' by the Rabhaman.

A few instances in Karlsson's work further testified to their distaste for the colonial authorities. In a village called Sissu-Jhomra, Dhansing Mech, age 100 (approx.) narrated that his father had told him that the Bhotias rule was better than that of the British.[13] He mentioned that,

> The Bhutia collectors came only once a year, collected eight rupees per family and left us to enjoy as much land as we could cultivate. The British came they spoke sweet words. They gave us protection no doubt but they increased the rents, introduced many laws and we gradually lost our lands and shifted from place to place. Now I have four acres of land that can hardly maintain my family.[14]

According to an estimate during the last hundred years or more about 50,000 acres of land were cleared to yield place to large and small tea estates leaving small patches of forest and paddy lands in between. The tea labourers bought many patches of land belonging to the Meches. The Meches gradually crossed the Balasan and the Mahananda and shifted to Baikunthpur forest in Jalpaiguri. A part of the Baikunthpur forest was subsequently acquired by some tea estates and a large number of immigrants took possession of the forest clearings which the Meches used for cultivating paddy. The low rent of the land attracted the migrants. A large number of Meches had to cross the Teesta and migrate to the Duars where fallow lands were plenty. As the Duars abounded in large tea estates, the Mech had to move further east upto the River Sankosh between Jalpaiguri and Assam.

D. Sunder mentioned a taluk named Totgaon in Chengmari pargana within tahasil Mynaguri at present under P.S. Mal (Jalpaiguri). It is situated on the eastern bank of the river Teesta near its confluence with a tributary, the river Leesh. Sunder recounted that the taluk was named after the Totos who used to reside there. Accounts point to the fact that three to four generations ago a considerable number of Totos lived in Western Duars. The whole area of the Western Duars was under Bhutan till 1865 and probably due to depredation of the Bhutias and malarious fever the Totos nearly disappeared. The small number that survived moved from place to place as a wandering tribe in search of a shelter. In the process, some of them were absorbed into the Mech tribe. A few who survived took shelter in the very secluded and healthier portion of a hill surrounded by deep wood where they confined themselves strictly within its limits (this at present is the Totopara area).

They practiced jhum cultivation and reared lac insects on black sal trees growing in the adjacent forest. Some of them corroborated that, in the past, they had extensive cultivation of lac which of late had dwindled. The little lac they obtained was exchanged for rice, salt or clothing in the nearest market. Orange trees perished, cotton growing too was abandoned.[15] Practically no industry existed barring weaving and spinning. During the rainy season when the outside food supply was totally severed their only means of sustenance was the succulent roots of a shrub growing wild in the forest called Simul Kanda.

With the rapid pace of reservation and a large chunk of their land being occupied by 'others' (new settlers such as Oraons, Santhals etc.), the old jhum cultivation had to be abandoned by many of the Totos. They could not raise sufficient food to maintain themselves in the plots of land allotted to some families. The Government was aware of the critical situation emerging for these shifting cultivators and wanted to compensate it, by setting aside land for them. For the first time the word compensation was found in the colonial repertoire. Settling nomadic people was a common colonial practice and besides evicting the shifting cultivators to facilitate forest operations and tea plantations was the simplest method of adjusting these 'disturbing elements'. Moreover, mobile populations were considered safety risks by most governments. The colony established somehow proved unsuccessful. Within a short span of time, most of the land reserved for the Meches and Garos had been taken over by others, as no special measures were taken to check such transfers. While probing into the years 1907-08 the colonial authorities found that all the Garos had left the colony and that half of the land in the colony were in hands of outsiders, mainly Oraons from the tea plantations.[16] The Mech and Garo colony was again brought into focus in connection to an additional forest reservation in 1917. Other than the colony, no other land was set aside or granted specifically to the indigenous shifting cultivators in Duars.[17] Adverse circumstances and decreasing access to the forest coaxed some of these indigenous communities to become agricultural labourers or adhiars, workers on rented land on a fifty-fifty basis, i.e., giving half the crop to the persons having land titles, and very few managed to secure jotes in their own name. Practically no Rabhas or Meches turned to the tea gardens for employment.[18] Besides, those who did, appeared not to have been permanently employed. Some of them lived on tea-garden lands, but only cultivated vacant land for themselves and restrained from contributing to the tea manufacturing process.[19]

It would be baffling to answer as to why these indigenous communities shunned the work in the tea gardens. Neither did the forest department, particularly in the late nineteenth century provide any job opportunities for them. Recruitment took place on the occasion of fighting forest fires, but on an irregular basis. The forest authorities often recruited labour gangs from outside, mainly Nepalis for the purpose. A few accounts would unravel their discomfiture at the hands of the forest department and tea plantations.[20]

Bijoy Narjinari, a Mech man (age 80 years) of village, Kumargram, mentioned that neither he nor his predecessors or his kin had ever worked in the tea gardens. The forest department recruited them as forced labourers for preparing the ground for plantation and tendering the new saplings. In lieu of his services the forest department permitted them to cultivate the land in between two rows of the plantation trees.[21] Another Mech man called Khagendra Mochary (age 78 years) of village Balapara residing in forest bustee (village), P.S. Hemaguri, recalled with a lot of disdain the work in tea garden and his disinterest for it. He mentioned that, " I have seen a tea garden but never had the opportunity nor desire to work in it."[22] He, however, confessed that he had worked as a forest labourer and so had his predecessors for which the forest department supposedly did not owe him anything.

Dinabandhu Basumata (age 98 years approx.) of Ghokshapara village converted to Christianity, ostracized by the Hinduised Meches, a substantial *jotedar*, but adhered to the traditional customs of weaving and bamboo constructions along with his labourers and small peasants. Habil Borgaon (age 78 years) of Ghokshapara village shunned the work of a forest labourer as well due to the prevalence of *begar* (forced labour) but had worked in the tea garden as a daily wage labourer driven by the vagaries of the floods. These accounts are further substantiated by the narratives accounts Karlssons' work portrayed as a Rabha man recounted their transition from nomads to settled forest villagers,

> Earlier we moved from place to place, breaking new land and cultivating (haipidan daboigi). Then Sunder sahib came and told us that we had to settle down and remain in one place. Other people, black-

> people, from the south had come here and were taking over the land. He said that the Government (Sarkar) had started to demarcate land, and in order to get some we had to there permanently. We didn't believe him. We asked, why should people want to come here, to the forest (jhar). At that time there were few people here. But we were wrong, Bengalis and other jatis came here, and land became scarce. Then when the service group came, they divided the land among the people who had settled down, and a demarcation line was made between what was going to be forest and what would be agricultural land. Most of the Kochas escaped to the north of the line, but some stayed to the south, and they also got land titles. Some were still saying that there was plenty of land and that the Kochas could continue to move from place to place in the forest. But after demarcation it became difficult for them. The forest now belonged to sarkar. Some Kochas then went east to search for land, but the forest was also demarcated there. Confused the Kochas started wandering around. Finally the Britishara (British people) said all right, you can stay in the forest, we will give you some land, but then you shall have to help us with the plantation work. The first plantation took place in 1915, and was done by the Kochas. It has been going on since then ...[23]

The establishment of forest villages was considered absolutely essential in order to ensure a permanent supply of labour. Forest official Shebbeare was assigned the task of restructuring the system of forest villages in view of the prevailing circumstances. According to him in 1894 the first labourers had been settled inside the reserved forests, but the early settlements for fire prevention were shortlived and by 1902 all of them were deserted. From 1904 onwards, it became regular policy in the Jalpaiguri Division to establish forest villages.[24] Similarly, in the

Buxa Division, most of the forest villages were established between the year 1905 and 1911. There was a phenomenal growth of forest villages during 1916-17, i.e. from 437 to 585 or about 34 per cent. In 1924, the Buxa Forest Division had 18 (permanent) forest villages and the number of houses was 410 while in the Jalpaiguri Forest Division there were 21 villages and 236 houses.

These relatively independent shifting cultivators were transformed into settled forest villagers under the hard rule of the Forest Department. With the loss of the jungle, which was either reserved, converted into tea gardens, or made into agricultural land, there not many options left open. Consequently, the forest villages were in a constant state of flux. Households and often entire villages were deserted while others came into being.[25] They expressed their displeasure about residing in a forest village in the following words, "When our predecessors never left behind precedents of such livelihood why should we?"[26]

The forest villagers' access to more permanent land or more labour days, preferably yearly employment was regarded as a pre-requisite for any real improvement of their economic situation. The Forest Department, however, differed. According to them, every labourer had already been provided with work for about seven months a year. The demand for additional land in the forest was far from consideration. It was simply ruled out on the basis that it would be illegal, since the Forest Department was not authorized to grant forest land or reserved forests, for agricultural or other non-forestry purposes.

To return to the question of legal status of the lands already possessed or cultivated by the tribals, the Forest Department considered these lands as leased or granted to the forest villagers in return for their services to the Forest Department, "the lease is only temporary, and the land remains the property of the state".[27] This was the position expressed in the forest official's general rhetoric, and in the land documents some of the forest villagers process till date. This position of the forest department was uncritically accepted by the post-colonial government as the policies of the colonial government were bequeathed to its successor. M.K.Raha pointed out that, "the land, the house and other constructions are not their own, but actually belong to the Forest Department of the State Government. The forest authority only permits them to enjoy these temporarily in exchange of their labour rendered to this department on year to year contract".[28]

The category 'forest village' was an administrative category and found its logical culmination in the Forest Jagir Village in the post-colonial period. Construction of *pucca* huts was initiated in 1947-48 and had continued till 1960-61. It was observed that the number of households increased by sixty-six per cent from 1970 onwards. The indigenous people distinctly distinguished between the British *Amol* (period) and the Bangla *Amol* and their displeasure with the latter period. As Indira Boshumata (70 years) narrated that,

> Earlier there were problems between Kochas and Bhutias, but later the British conquered the Bhutias. The British themselves were later conquered by the Bengalis. Now Kochas have started demanding their own country again. But this is only possible for Kochas in Assam, where there are many educated people. Here we lack educated people who could organize such a movement. All the Bengalis, who live in the towns- Alipur, Cooch Behar, Birpara - are rich, they come from outside. We all the hasong marab (original inhabitants) are poor and live in the villages.[29]

Critical remarks about the post independent government or Bengali rule (as they often referred to it) often addressed the condition of the labourers and how the plantations were managed. The following account by a Mech man, Abia

Mochary, (age 80) and his wife (age 68 approx.), Fulosree Mochary is an interesting one, she confesses,

> Being the village headman's wife I was spared the duties of a forest labourer and so was my husband. Despite the hapless poverty-stricken condition we never felt the urge to work in the tea gardens.[30]

A remuneration in lieu of their labour was never considered essential by the forest department. Men were recruited for lumbering operations while the women prepared the ground for the plantations which included weeding, preparing the soil and sowing the saplings. Both involved extensive manual labour.

Karlsson's work focuses on similar narratives and the despondency that loomed large particularly over the post-colonial period. Referring to an account in his work he quotes Dhansing Mech,

> During British time there was peace in the forest. There was no shortage of food or other things, like there is now. Everything was better for us. But we also worked harder. We could plant rice and vegetables and other things, like there is now. Everything was restricted in the forest. If the British had remained here, I think the Kochas would still be ruling over the forests. But they were forced to leave. The British liked us Kochas. Before they left they told us that we should become Christians and occupy land outside the forest and get it registered, since many people would come here from the south. We didn't follow their instructions. Now dark times are coming, both for the forest and for us in the forest villages. So many people came from outside to take timber and firewood. The forest disappears. And then it will become difficult for us to find food, build houses and get employment (meaning work in the plantations). Today only Bengalis are employed by the Forest Department, earlier it was

> only Kochas and Nepalis who patrolled the forest together with the British.[31]

Their marginalization they felt turned a full circle with the introduction of the Forest Jagir Village and their discrimination as registered villagers or faltu (unregistered) villagers, the latter being subject to evictions was evident.[32] In 1969 the North Bengal Forest Villagers and Jagir Cultivators Union was formed. In 1970 they struck work and a charter of seventeen demands were put forward, including the abolition of the *taungya* system, minimum land holdings of fifteen *bighas* for every family, year round work with a daily wage and a regulated, six hour work a day, a new housing programme and proper education.[33] The strike continued for a year and a half. This movement was described as a great success as begari labour or unpaid labour in vogue since colonial times was abolished. After that the Forest Department had to pay a fixed daily salary for all the work in the forest. As Shaonshri Karji of village Kamakhyaguri, corroborates that,

> Being illiterate we had been cheated by the Mahajan and we were forced to go back to a life of nomadism. We became forest labourers with a daily wage of Rs. 16 or more. Sundays were holidays but we didn't turn to the tea garden for work.[34]

Nripendra Kumar Gabur (age 78) of village Domohni, P.S.Kalchini even spoke of participating in 'tenders' announced by the government for cutting of trees in the 1970s.[35] He confessed that given an opportunity they would work in the tea gardens. Ansik Basumata, age 65, was originally a resident of Kokrajhar district, Assam. He decided to work as a forest labourer once wages were fixed, however, meagre in the beginning. Some lamented their loss of land to the tea gardens and other public and defence purposes like the Hasimara airbase.[36]

The forest villagers' access to more permanent land or more labour days, preferably yearly employment was regarded as a pre-requisite for any real improvement of their economic situation. The forest department, however, differed. It was simply ruled out on grounds of legality forest department being unauthorized to grant forest land or reserved forests for agricultural or non-forestry purposes. With the implementation of the taungya system, these shifting cultivators who had become a left over population with no place in the new colonial plan, suddenly became a crucial asset to the forest department. This heralded an era of collaboration from conflict. However, since collaboration was imposed from above the life of a forest villager and that of a captive labourer did not augur well for a new venture. This structure being accommodated with minor variations during the post-colonial phase was also confronted with similar difficulties. At times the latter phase was resented more than its precedent. A populist approach gained currency only in the latter half of the twentieth century with the commencement of social forestry projects and joint forest management.

The biography of the Botanical Garden was a forecast of the predominant commercial interests prevalent and found its reflection in the formulation of colonial forest policy. Its Implementation perpetrated a saga of displacement. Memoirs of the displaced constructs histories of the marginalized people. Their discontent with the British Raj permeated into the latter period which failed to appreciate their aspirations. A joint collaborative endeavour, despite its shortcomings, had been initiated in the 1970s following a bout of unrests. Participation in tenders for lumbering operations announced by the government was undoubtedly a welcome change leaving for posterity to judge its constructive outcome.

Notes & Refenrences

1. Mark Harrison, "The Calcutta Botanic Garden and the Wider World, 1817-46", in Uma Dasgupta (ed.) *Science and Modern India : An Institutional History, 1784-1947*, Vol. XIV, Part IV, Centre for Studies in Civilisation, Pearson, 2011, p. 235.
2. Sir George King 'History of the Institution' in *Bengal Administration Report, 1886-87*, Bengal Secretariat Book Depot, Calcutta, 1888, pp. 112-11.
3. *Bengal Administration Report, 1886-87*, Calcutta, 1888, p. 112.
4. George King, "History of the Institution", op. cit., p. 112.
5. Ibid., p. 112.
6. Richard Grove, Richard H.Grove, *Green Imperialism: Colonial Expansion, Tropical Island Edens and the Origins of Environmentalism, 1600-1860*, Cambridge University Press, Delhi: Foundation Books, 1995, p. 25.
7. George King, "History of the Institution", op. cit., p. 112.
8. Ibid., p. 113.
9. Richard Grove, *Green Imperialism : Colonial Expansion, Tropical Island Edens and the Origins of Environmentalism, 1600-1860*, op. cit., p. 30.
10. George. W. King, *History of the Institution*, op. cit., p. 113.
11. *Bengal Administration Report, 1886-87*, Bengal Secretariat Book Depot, Calcutta, 1887, p. 27.
12. B.G. Karlsson, *Contested Belonging : An Indigenous People's Struggle for Forest Identity in Sub-Himalayan Bengal*, (Lund University, Department Sociology, 1997), pp. 90-91.
13. B.G. Karlsson, *Contested Belonging*, op. cit., p. 91.
14. Ibid., p. 91.
15. Bimalendu Majumdar, *The Totos*, Calcutta, 1998, p. 12.
16. J.F. Gruning, *Eastern Bengal and Assam District Gazetteers – Jalpaiguri*, Allahabad, 1911, p. 20.
17. Ibid., p. 21.
18. C.C. Sanyal, *The Meches and Totos of North Bengal*, Calcutta, 1973, p. 30.
19. Ibid., p. 30.
20. During my field survey I interviewed a number of people from the Mech community and was accompanied by my student Shri Santana Mochary, himself a Mech.
21. *Progress Report of Forest Administration, 1915*, Calcutta, 1915, p. 10.
22. Khagendra Mochary's displeasure with the work in the tea-garden.
23. B.G. Karlsson, *Contested Belonging*, op. cit., p. 124.

24. Progress Report of Forest Administration, 1905, Calcutta 1905, p. 10
25. J.F. Gruning, *Eastern Bengal and Assam District Gazetteers*, op. cit., p. 25.
26. Major R.C.Money, 'Levy of Permit and Licence fees from Bhutias and Nepalese Resident in - (Head) Mis. (Col) 11, Proceedings', 3 March, 1876, p. 15, as cited in Santana Mochary's M.Phil dissertation (unpublished), "Oupanibeshik Shashonkale Mech Janajatir Jibon O Samajer Ruprekha, 1865-1950", p. 43.
27. M.K.Raha, *The Rabhas of West Bengal*, Calcutta, 1967, p. 30.
28. Ibid., p. 31.
29. B.G. Karlsson, *Contested Belonging*, op. cit., p. 129.
30. Abia Mochary of village Domohoni, never felt the urge to work in a tea garden.
31. B.G. Karlsson, *Contested Belonging*, op. cit., p. 130.
32. Ibid, p. 132.
33. *Progress Report of Forest Administration in the Lower Provinces of Bengal, 1968-69*, Calcutta, 1969, p. 30.
34. Shaonsri Karji of village Kamakhyguri was optimistic when he mentioned a daily age scheme to me.
35. Nripendra Kumar Gabur, of village Domohoni, was excited about participating in the tenders announced by the Government.
36. Land acquisition for public purposes is controversial till date and points to the much debated Land Acquisition Bill of 1891.

A Short Biography of Tan-Yunshan: Retrieving from Archival Documents

Dr. Arpita Bose

Tan-Yunshan was a Buddhist Chinese scholar who was well known for his association with late poet Rabindranath Tagore and also for building *Cheena Bhawan* (Chinese Hall) at Visva Bharati University, Santiniketan. He was particularly conspicuous in history for his role in developing Sino-Indian relationship[1] in the twentieth century. Former President of India, Mr. K.R. Narayanan, in a message on the birth-centenary of Tan-Yunshan mentioned him as a Chinese scholar 'who personified the deep and abiding ties of civilizations of India and China.' He developed close ties with the leaders of both the countries, India and China during the Second World War and secured Chinese state funding for Cheena Bhawan, the first Sino-Indological institute ever established in India.

Except Prof. Tan's own writings[2] there are very few scholarly publications which informed us about his ideology and illustrious career. A commemorative volume[3] of the birth centenary of Prof. Tan-Yunshan, edited by his worthy son Prof. Tan-Chung, however, contains some valuable essays on his historical role as cultural ambassador in India and speaks a lot on his thoughts and mission in developing Sino-Indian relationship. A good number of scholars has also recorded their personal memories with Prof. Tan and have expressed their tribute to him in this volume. Very recently Brian Tsui[4] discussed about Tan's success as a diplomat and as an institute builder. Brian also tries to throw light on his idea of Pan-Asianism and shifting dynamics of the Pan-Asianist movement. The present article seeks to portray a biographical sketch of Tan Yunshan (1898-1983) as an academic and his activities in India based on the Government reports preserved in the West Bengal State Archives, Kolkata.

Tan's Arrival in India

The turning point of Tan's life was his meeting with world-famous poet Rabindranath Tagore, in Singapore. After four years of intellectual association with him, Tagore discovered a true Chinese ideological companion in Tan Yunshan. He was invited to come to India by the poet to teach at Visva Bharati in 1927.This offer seemed an opportunity of life-time by Tan. He did not want to miss the chance to visit India. He wrote, 'I always feel that India is a place one must not miss it' (Yunshan-Tan). However owing to the non-availability of suitable India-China air transport during those days, Prof. Tan[5] had decided to follow the footsteps of famous Chinese traveler Xuan Zhang, popularly known in history as Hiuen Tsang. He took a boat trip to reach India along the maritime Silk Route.[6] He came to India in 1928. Intelligence Branch Report (Hence forth referred as IB) also informs us that he first came to be noticed in India in November 1928. A letter written by him to R.C. Chang, Secretary of all India Kuomintang party, Kolkata intercepted by the Intelligence Department also confirms this information.[7]

Tan's Early Life and Career

Prof. Tan was reported to have been born in 1898[8] though Archival sources indicate his birth in 1900, at a province called Cha Ling, Hunan. He belonged to the famous Hakka group. He was a class mate of Mao-Zedong in school days. After graduating from a Teacher Training College in Hunan, he continued his post-graduate research at Chun Shan University under the supervision of Tsai -Chieh-Min. After meeting with Tagore he decided to do research on Sino-Indian cultural relationship. His research work on the subject 'The World Calendar and its Reform' proposes improvement in the calendar system. He had started his professional career as a teacher, journalist and a publisher in Shanghai, Singapore, Rangoon and British colony in Malaya. He offered his valuable service as a teacher for the betterment of education of the overseas Chinese people in Malaya since 1924.[9]

Tan's Philosophical and Political Ideology

Prof. Tan was a staunch follower of Buddhism since 1924. He was converted to Buddhism by Chinese master Taixu[10] who was an ardent advocate of Buddhism in Republican China. Taixu's activities were very popular among the intellectuals of both the right and left wing groups in China.[11] Tan used his concept of Buddhism to analyze the relevance of Sino-Indian interactions to a world fraught by the spiritual crisis created by liberal capitalism. Besides being thoroughly conversant with the philosophies of Confucius and Buddha he had also interests in modern science and literature, Oriental and European alike. In his later years he became interested in Yoga.[12] Tan was deeply impressed by Gandhi's principal of non-violence, anti-colonialism and concept of social movement. He was a main interpreter of Gandhi's political programme which appeared in the journal *New Asia*, a house publication of New Asia Society.[13] He was interested in the works and writings of other spiritual leaders like Sri Aurobindo, Acharya Kripalani, Vinoba Bhave, and Swami Sivananda. He maintained regular correspondence with them and also visited Aurobindo Asrama at Pondichery on a number of occasions. He also maintained contacts with several other people interested in developing Sino-Indian cultural relationship.[14]

Prof. Tan had his respective political ideology and affiliation. From his early boyhood he was familiar with the changing political and cultural scenario of China that began to manifest particularly since the forties of the last century. According to the Indian official records he was formerly a member of the Chinese Communist Party and subsequently turned to be a zealous Kuomintang worker in India.[15] But Brian Tsui mentioned that Tan never was a member of the Chinese Communist Party or Kuomintang. He pointed out that Tan never involved himself in active politics and preferred to stay away from organized party politics.[16] He joined politics after his association with Tagore when he was teaching at Visva Bharati. As a journalist and newspaper printer he was aware about Tagore's controversial visit to China in 1923. Though a supporter of Modern Vernacular Movement, Tan was neither an activist nor a member of the new radical cultural groups. He was not happy with the progress of social radicalism of his time the advocates of which mostly gathered around Marxist Study group. He did not participate in the May Fourth Movement in China. He did not hold any important position in any institution under Chian kai Shek regime in China. Actually he was a marginalized academic who was socially and geographically removed from the centers of gravity. His peripheral intellectual status actually made him an ideal operator of Sino-Indian interaction in lieu of State to State Diplomacy.[17] He often preferred to be treated as a mediator of educational and cultural relation between the two countries.

Relation with K.M.T and Nanking Authority

According to Indian official reports, Tanyun Shan was a zealous K.M.T worker in India. He took keen interest in politics and worked for the betterment of Sino-Indian relationship which used to be looked upon with suspicion during those days.[18] He had close contact with several prominent K.M.T leaders of Calcutta such as Li-Wei-Pin, Wong- C-Yuan etc. He participated in all the party programs held in India.[19]

In 1929 Prof. Tan attended a meeting at Chinese Theatre in Central Avenue, Calcutta organized by the Overseas Chinese Kuomintang Party of India to celebrate the eighteenth anniversary[20] of the birth of the Republic of China. He also delivered a lecture there. He reviewed the history of Chinese revolution and paid rich tribute to the contribution of Dr. Sun-Yat-Sen for facilitating Chinese liberation and independence. He pointed out that the imperialist powers had attempted to overthrow nationalism in Korea, Indo-China and India, but it still survived in these countries. He advised Asiatic countries to follow the example of Japan which was the only independent country of Asia at that time.[21]

Tan-Yunshan's cordial relationships with Nanking began as late as 1930 when he joined a delegation of Nationalist State Representative on a mission to Lasha. Tan played a pivotal role as an unofficial diplomat as Chiang Kaishek's envoy Xie Guoliang died from illness before setting foot on Tibet. Tan successfully conveyed the message of Chinese Premier Chiang- Kai sekh to Dalai Lama and send another report to Nanking where he mentioned that it seems very disgraceful for Chinese nationals to visit Tibbet via British India. He believed that Tibet was an integral part of China.[22]

In an interview published in the Chinese Journal of India in 1945 he requested the overseas Chinese to give their full support to the general Issimo and the K.M.T. He assigned the Chinese internal political instability to mal-functioning of a comparatively small group of disgruntled politicians the advantage of which was being taken over by a large group of ill-informed foreigners were making most of it.[23]

Nanking authority appointed him as a Chinese Educational and Cultural Representative in India in 1948 and entrusted the duty to improve the cultural relationship between the two nations. The four Chinese schools in Calcutta Mei-Kuang, Chien-Kuo, Pei-Mei and Chung-Hua Middle had jointly organized a reception party to celebrate his new appointment as Cultural and Educational representative of China and to appreciate excellent services rendered by him.

Li-Wei-Pin, a prominent K.M.T leader in Calcutta requested Tan Yunshan at a very crucial situation to take active part in politics on behalf of the Chinese nationalists. But Prof. Tan did not accept his offer and informed Mr. Li-Wei-Pin that he was not in a position to take active part in politics due to his present circumstances. The real fact is that he decided to support Mao-tse Tung. He gave suggestion to him that it was the duty of the overseas Chinese to remain united for the purpose of rescuing China and Chinese people. They should try to eschew violence in connection with Chinese politics as violence begets confusion and chaos and would benefit none. Gradually his bonding with the Nationalist camp waned in course of time since the 1950s.[24]

Prof. Tanyun Shan's Role in Indian Politics

Tan-Yunshan was an active participator in Indian political affairs. His cultural activities had intermingled with K.M.T activities. He was not only a cultural representative in India but he appeared as a definite politician. According to the official records, "he is a first class example of the Chinese who have condemned the British, a man working for his Government under the cloth of missionary or cultural activity." He also championed the case of India's independence. He wrote an article entitled "Declare India Independent Immediately and Free Immediately" published in 'The Hindustan Standard' on 8th October 1942 where he had appealed to the U.K pointing out that for every body's sake she should free India immediately. A telegram was also sent to Chiang- Kaisekh to intervene in the matter of release of Mahatma Gandhi on February 1943. He also staged a 'sympathy with Gandhi' demonstration when Tagore visited to Poona to see the Mahatma.[25]

Prof. Tan and Various Organization

Prof. Tan had diverse and wide contacts. He was associated with various organization viz. 'Sino-Indian Cultural Society', 'The Peoples Foreign Relation Association', 'The Indo— Chinese Friendship Association', 'The Overseas Chinese Syndicate', 'The Indian Brotherhood League', and 'The International Anti Aggression Movement'. The Sino-Indian Cultural Society played a very significant role to bring these two great civilizations into close contact during the colonial period. According to him, "for centuries China and India had helped each other in many ways and they together bring the world back from the brink of war to peace". The Sino-Indian Cultural Society was also supported by the Kuomintang.[26] Tan-Yunshan was a founder member of the Sino-Indian Cultural Society. It was organized in 1931 in Nanking after his arrival in China from India. In 1934 he again returned to India and an Indian branch of the Sino-Indian Cultural Society was established at VisvaBharati, Santiniketan, Bolepur. RabindraNath Tagore played a very important role in organizing the Sino-Indian Cultural Society. He also acted as its president in India. According to Prof Tan, "this was done even more smoothly than in China." The objectives of the society were to establish linkages between the civilizations of the two countries, to foster cultural exchanges, cultivate friendship and to promote a sense of fraternity among people of two countries.[27] After formation of the society Prof. Tan returned to China. But again in 1936 he came to India for the third time along with one lakh books which had been donated by the Sino-Indian Cultural Society and the national Government of China. Dr. Tan received a fairly large subsidy from the International Propaganda Department of Central Kuomintang in Chungking, China to promote Sino-Indian relation. In March 1944 the Ministry of Education in China announced in a message to the society that they had sanctioned fifty scholarships to Indian students which was reciprocated by the grant of scholarships to Chinese students at Santiniketan.[28] In December 1944 the 10th anniversary of the Sino-Indian Cultural Society was celebrated with much fanfare at Santiniketan.

The Indian branch of the Peoples Foreign Relation Association was opened in Calcutta in February 1944 with Chow Hsiang kuang , a student of Cheena Bhavan as its general secretary. This is also a Kuomintang sponsored organization. Prof. Tan was closely associated with this association. Among others Consul general C.J. Pao, Wang Fu Shih were also associated with this organization.[29]

The idea to form the Indo-Chinese Friendship Association was first mooted by Dr. C.J. Pao, the then Chinese Consul General of India in 1942. But it didn't become successful until 1948. The Communist Party of West Bengal had been endeavoring for the inauguration of the long deferred Indo-Chinese Friendship Association. In January 1948 Prof. Hiren Mukharjee, Gopal Halder, Prof. Niren Roy and Prof. K.P. Chatterji took some initiative to give a shape to the association. But this communist move did not meet success as Mr. Liao, the editor of the Chinese Journal of India, Calcutta, suspecting a communist game in it dropped the matter. Then Prof. K.P. Chatterji and Kalidas Nag went to Bolepur and discussed the whole matter afresh with Prof. Tan Yunshan. Prof. Tan created a pressure on Mr. Liao to inaugurate the Indo-Chinese Friendship Association. He assured that the Communist

Party would not be able to sabotage their objects namely "Indo-Chinese Cordial Entente and anti-Communist Front".[30] He also established "Indian Brotherhood League" with the help of Tai- Chi-Tao. Mr. Tai- Chi- Tao gave necessary assistance when "The Indian Brotherhood League" came into being in September 1943.[31]

Tan as a Founder of Cheena Bhavan

The Department of Chinese Studies popularly known as Cheena Bhavan with Tan as its head was established at Santiniketan in 1936. By that time Tan visited India thrice as a traveller or cultural representative of China. Cheena Bhavan had received students from foreign lands such as China, Srilanka and Java. Apart from performing administrative duties Professor Tan used to deliver lectures to Chinese students in Cheena Bhavan. It is necessary to mention in this context that the idea to establish a Chinese Department at Visva Bharati, Santiniketan was first conceived by Rabindranath Tagore when he led the first Indian Cultural Mission in China in 1924 on an invitation from the Lecture Association of Peking. Tagore expressed his idea but the proposal could not be worked out immediately.

Tan Yunshan had a very friendly relation with Tai-Chi-Tao, of the Examination Council and Chen Li Fu of the Department of Education of Chinese Govt. These two officials had influenced the Propaganda Department of the Kuomintang to subsidize Tan Yunshan activities in Santiniketan. Tai Chi Tao was mainly responsible for raising the funds to build the Chinese Hall or Cheena Bhavan and was the main sponsor of Prof. Tan. He visited Santiniketan when he came to India in 1940 along with all the members of his 'Good Will Mission of Burma and India'[32] and donated seven thousand rupees to Visva Bharati for various objects. In 1941 Tai-chi remitted rupees three thousand for extension of the library of the Chinese Hall at Visva-Bharati. Tai-Chi-Tao also donated ten thousand rupees for rural upliftmen works organized by Visva Bharati and for building dormitories as well as for the improvement of Cheena Bhavan. In 1943 when Madam Chiang Kai Shek came to Calcutta, Tanyun Shan sent an invitation to her through the Chinese Consul General to visit Santiniketan. He wished to use her influence in bringing about an agreement with the authorities so that the proposed work might be started at the Cheena Bhavan.

As a director of Cheena Bhavan, Tan got his salary from the Education Ministry of Chunking, China. He also received about two hundred rupees per month from Visva-Bharati. The whole expense of Chinese students at Cheena Bhavan including their food, lodging etc., was borne out by the Educational Ministry Chungking, China. The amount was sent to Prof. Tan, Director of Cheena Bhavan. He spent the money keeping in mind the interest of students. The monthly subsidy granted to Tan was thirty six thousand dollar per annum which at the current rate of exchange was equal to rupees nine thousand. Out of this subsidy he had to pay rupees forty per month as scholarships to two Chinese students sponsored by the Chinese Government at Santiniketan. After paying the expense for maintaining the Chinese Hall and Sino-Indian Cultural Society from this fund rest of the money was retained by him. According to a secret report it is difficult to know how Tan Yunshan disposes of the sum of money he received. But it is clear that his financial condition was quite good. The secret report also reveals the fact that the Chinese people living in Kolkata were rather in dark about Tan's activities in Santiniketan. However his relationship with the poet remained cordial as ever and he also maintained a good relationship with other nationalist leaders of India.[33]

Tan Yunshan again prayed to the Chinese Nationalist Government to increase the grant for the Chinese student at Cheena Bhavan, Santiniketan in 1945. Dr. H.H. Kung, Minister of Finance in the Chinese Government, had informed him that owing to the strict control of foreign exchange Government could do nothing at present to increase the grant for students at Santiniketan.[34]

The Cheena Bhavan of Santiniketan was experiencing financial difficulties since 1949. The financial help from the Chinese Nationalist Government was not coming regularly due to civil war. So in that context after the advent of the communist regime in China, Professor Tan-Yunshan decided to appeal to the Government of China to continue the annual grant to the Visva Bharati. Since 1950, the Peking Government authorized the Chinese Consul General, Calcutta to pay the annual subsidy to the authorities of Visva Bharati.

Tanyun Shan and United Chinese Corporation

Prof. Tan was taking keen interest in the affairs of the United Chinese Corporation. This firm was engaged in illicit exchange business in India. Chin-Chang-Cheng @ K.C. Chin the proprietor of the United Chinese Corporation had personal connections with Prof. Tanyun Shan, Li-Wei –Pin and others K.M.T leaders. Mr. Li-Wei-Pin had introduced him with Prof. Tan. Chin had been detained at Kunming for his black market activities in 1945. He was however released through the intervention of Tan. As a gesture of appreciation of Tan's services Chin had adopted Tan's youngest son as his sole heir. Chan was also childless. Tan was also the sole trustee of Chin's interest in the United China Corporation.[35]

Anglo-Japanese War

Tan-Yunshan had played a significant role for achieving the cooperation of Indian leaders and intellectuals during the war against Japan war in 1930's. But in the early stage this task was not so easy for him to win the hearts of the Indians to oppose the Japanese aggression against China. Indian leaders had sympathy on Japan since 1905 when they defeated Russia. Even his Indian sponsor Poet Rabindranath Tagore was very close to Japanese people and had good feelings on Japan. Tagore's close associate Kalidas Nag was also pro Japanese. Subhas Chandra Bose also took the Japanese help to form the Indian National Army and extended his support to the 'Great East Asian Sacred War' lunched by Japan. In this context Chungking authority utilizing the position of Prof. Tan in India entrusted the responsibility to create anti-Japanese consciousness against the attack on China. Prof. Tan had delivered a series of lectures all over India on the atrocities committed by the Japanese in China, and also described about the bravery of the Chinese soldiers in fighting against the Japanese. Under his influence Rabindranath Tagore exchanged correspondence in 1938 with Jap poet Noguchi where he mentioned that China is unconquerable. All India National Congress adopted a resolution on China in1938 at Haripura, Gujarat and send its deepest sympathy to the people of China.[36]

All India National Congress also expressed its admiration for the heroic struggle of the Chinese soldiers. As marks of their sympathy with the Chinese people the Congress called upon the people of India to refrain from purchasing Japenese goods. Pandit Jaawharlal Nheru wrote that " the recent events in China shocked the people of India and all our sympathies are with the people of China" .Even Subhas Chandra Bose also expressed his sympathy to their struggle in 1938.[37]

Tai Chi Tao, of Chinese Government and Chen-Lu-Fu, Minister of Education of the Chinese Government were greatly impressed with Tan's successful attempts to foster friendship between the two countries as well as gaining sympathy for China in her great struggle with Japan.[38] According to Hung Chih Lien, "the Japanese conspiracy in mobilizing the upper class Indian intellectuals towards their side was defeated or at least neutralized".[39]

But it is quite surprising that as per the report of secret official documents , "... beyond building the Chinese Hall and getting a few Chinese scholar from China to study at Santiniketan, Tan Yun actually has not done much work with the exceptions that he also lecture for a fortnight at the Andhara University".[40] It is recorded that "his close association with Dr. Tagore has naturally brought him into contact with prominent Indian leaders such as Gandhi and J. Nehru. On the rare occasions that he meets these leaders are of course the usual pleasantries concerning the close relationship between India and China and Tan-Yunshan's part in promoting the exchange of culture between the two people and the building of the Chinese Hall with its valuable books". According to this report Tan-Yunshan had capitalized the press reports in this connection and sent them to his Chinese sponsors. As a result of publicity they instruct the Publicity Department of K.M.T to subsidize Prof. Tan.

Relation with Communist China

The communist government of China also tried to utilize Prof. Tan's influence and popularity to establish their stronghold among the overseas Chinese in India and earned the sympathy of the Indian leaders. Prof. Tan also expressed his desire to support Mao-Tse-Tung. The pro-Communist students at Santiniketan had whole heartedly supported Prof. Tan.[41] He was reported to have developed pro-communist leaning from the latter part of 1949. He also maintained close contact with the Indian Communist. Prof. Chang Ching of Peking and Mr. Chang Hsiu Feng teacher of the Haing Hsiu Feng High school visited Santiniketan to meet Prof. Tan for the purpose of establishing cordial relation between the Cheena Bhavan on the one hand and the Chinese Embassy and the Chinese Consulate on the other. According to Shih Hsiu Lu, a student in the Cheena

Bhaban Mr. Chang Hsiu Feng and Prof. Chang Ching took this initiative in bringing about these two parties with a view to propagating the new thought as well as the new policy of the Republic of China. Even Prof. Chang Ching requested him to persuade the overseas Chinese youth and students in India to send telegram endorsing their allegiance to the Chinese Communist Government.

Naturally now the question arises why did Prof. Tan suddenly wish to support his classmate Mao? A man like Dr. Tanyun Shan didn't take this decision to support the Chinese communist party suddenly. His mental preparation to support Chinese Communist Party had been started since his return from China in June 1949. He began to criticize nationalist government in various issues viz. inflation, poor economic condition of the people, etc. According to him there were many able and honest men in the K.M.T Government but as a whole it was corrupt and inefficient. He explained that the Chinese people who had suffered much from the civil war wanted peace and unity for China. It was not of much concern to them which party was in power. But as a cultural representative he did not forget to mention that educational and cultural institution in both K.M.T and C.C.P occupied areas were carrying their activities despite tremendous difficulties. This proved that people remain loyal to their own culture. The usual financial help from the Chinese Nationalist Government was not coming due to break out of civil war in 1949. Prof. Tan faced great financial difficulties. He had to borrow money from his friends to meet his own expenses. Considering this situation it seems wise to Prof. Tan to express his allegiance towards Chinese communist to overcome the financial difficulties. Surprisingly after Tanyun Shan's desire to support Mao, Peking Govt. authorized to the Chinese Consul General, Calcutta to pay the annual subsidy to the VisvaBharati authority through the subject.

The Chinese scholars of Viswa-Bharati did not strictly follow the rules and regulation of the country. Since then the Indian authorities had lost some confidence in Prof. Tan. According to the Intelligence Branch report Cheena Bhavan at Santiniketan became a communist den under the supervision of Prof. Tan.[42]

His relation with Peoples Republic of China became more friendly and strong since the year 1956. He began to participate regularly at the celebration of Chinese Republic Day, organized by Chinese Consul General, Calcutta instead of joining Double Ten Day celebration. On behalf of the Chinese Consul General, Calcutta in a meeting he urged to the local Chinese to forge unity for the welfare of the main land China. He did not have any faith on the two Chinese nations (Beijing and Taiwan) theory. He was a strong supporter of United China under communist regime. Chou Enlai and Maotse Tung invited Prof. Tan to visit China in 1956. In response to this invitation Tanyun Shan and his daughter Tan Wen left Calcutta for China on 15th September 1956. On the eve of his journey Liu-Yu-Feng, the then Chinese Consul General of Calcutta and Chen-Lin-Hu, a prominent member of Chinese Communist Party arranged a special dinner party for him. After his arrival in China he wrote a letter to Chinese Consul General, Calcutta expressing his gratitude for arranging his journey to China. In a public meeting arranged on December 1956 at Hsing Hua High school, Calcutta he addressed the local Chinese residents. He narrated his experience and praised the Communist regime in China. During this time he also attended a party arranged at Rajbhavan, Calcutta in the honour of Chinese Prime Minister Chou-En-Lai.

According to a secret report dated 14th January 1958 he had been appointed as a representative of the People's political Consultative Committee, China and he had been receiving an allowance of rupees two thousand per month from the Chinese Consulate Calcutta since his visit to China in 1956. The Chinese Consulate, Calcutta also issued a cheque of rupees one thousand four hundred forty only in the name of his daughter Miss. Tan Wen as scholarship. During the middle of the March 1961, the Chinese Consul General again issued a cheque of rupees two thousand and eighty as scholarship in favour of his children Tan Wen and Tan Yuen. These were his rewards for showing loyalty to the Chinese Communist Party and the Peoples Republic of China.

Prof. Tan visited China with Red passport in September 1958. He was invited by the General Overseas Chinese Affairs Commission in connection with the Chinese National Day celebration and for lessening the strained relation between India and China. During this visit he also met with Chou Enlai and Indian ambassador posted in China. During this period of growing tension between India and China Tan used to make regular correspondence with the Chinese premier. He gave suggestion to the Chinese Premier to strengthen cultural ties with India by organizing Rabindra centenary. This cultural relation was the main domain of Prof Tan and he did not miss any chance to utilize this issue for his personal benefit.[43]

During 1960 Professor Tan- Yunshan purchased in the name of his wife a plot of land measuring about four bighas at Santiniketan to settle their permanently. The Indian Government did not raise any objection to Prof. Tan's acquiring this land in Birbhum, particularly in view of his association with poet Rabindranath Tagore. It indicates that he became able to recover his financial condition since his close association with the Communist.[44]

Tan after Sino-Indian Conflict

The border skirmish with China in 1962 also proved a turning point again in Tan's career. He seemed helpless and devastated. The ties between these two old civilizations were totally collapsed and co-operation was stopped. These two were the main elements of Prof. Tan's concept of Pan Asianist movement. His role as a mediator of Sino-

Indian friendship was no longer necessary. His Sino-Indian Friendship Association lost its importance. Questions were also raised at the parliament of India regarding the activities of Tan. Contemporary Indian magazine and newspapers repeatedly pointed out that he was a Chinese spy and raised allegation that the Public Service Commission, an important branch of the Indian Government became an agency of Chinese agents due to his influence upon the officers of the Intelligence, Home Department, Information and Broadcasting. In spite of that he had cordial relation with Indian leaders and also maintained his close relation with China. Chinese officers from Chinese embassy, New Delhi used to visit Santiniketan regularly. In March 1963 he went to Delhi in connection with organizing a peace march. However in India Tan's position was always safe and secured. His eldest son Tan Chun was appointed as a lecturer in the School of Foreign Language under the Ministry of Defense and his other son Tan Lee was also associated with Regional Town Planning Association.[45]

Conclusion

Tanyun Shan spend maximum time of his life in India. He was the icon of the patriotic Overseas Chinese group. He decided to live in India permanently since 1960 but didn't apply for citizenship. After his retirement from the post of principal of Cheena Bhavan, Visva Bharati he donated his property to the university and went to Bodh Gaya. He started preparation for establishing his dream project the World Buddha Academy at Gaya. He died there in 1983. Prof. Tan's close association with poet Rabindranath Tagore helped him to earn good reputation and brought him to the close contact of the Indian intellectuals. Thus he became a public figure at the stage of Asian geo-politics. He was quite famous for his ideas of universal brotherhood and Pan-Asianism. He represented a good mix of a successful diplomat, institution builder, good teacher and a clever politician.

Notes & Refenrences

1. I.B.File No-120/41, Prof. Tan Yunshan, West Bengal State Archives.
2. His English writings are *Modern China, The Cultural Relationship between China and India, China, India and the Second World War* etc. His works on Chinese are *A Journey Around India, More about India, Tagore and the Sino-Japanese War, Indian Autonomy – A Translation from Gandhi, Modern Chinese Politics, Economics and Sociology, the World Calendars and its Reform, India's Sympathy towards our War of Resistance, Sea Side Poems* etc.
3. Tan Chung edited, (1999), *In The Footsteps of Xuanzang: Tan-Yun-Shan and India*, Gyan Publishing, New Delhi. This commemoration volume was published in two different languages i.e., Chinese and English. The Chinese version was published by Chinese University of Hong Kong.
4. Brian Tsui (2010), *The Plea for Asia-Tan Yunshan :Pan Asianism and the Sino-Indian Relations*, China Report, Vol-46 (4), pp. 353-370.
5. Tan is described as modern Hieun Tsang by the Chinese people. As Hiuen Tsang spent a considerable part of his life in learning Buddhism and stayed in India. Similarly Prof. Tan had done to promote Chinese studied in India and spread Indian thoughts in China through various means.
6. Hung Chih Lien (2005), 'Turning Point of India China Relations in the twentieth Century: The Linkage Role of Tan-Yunshan', in M.Thampi (ed.), *India and China in Colonial World*, Social Science Press, New Delhi.
7. Ibid, I.B. File 120/41.
8. *Gazeteer of Chaling County* recorded that Tan Yunshan was born in 1898.
9. Ibid, I.B. File 120/41.
10. Taixu was deeply involved in the republican revolutionary movement and his eclectic propaganda helped to bring together two ideological groups of Faxing School and Henri Bergson's vitalism.
11. Ibid, Tsui Brain: 210:356.
12. Ibid, I.B. File: 120/ 41.
13. Ibid.
14. Tan-Lee, (1999), 'Life Sketch of Tanyun Shan ',Tan Chun et. al edited, *In The Footsteps of Xuanzang: Tan-Yun-Shan and India*, Gyan Publishing, New Delhi.pp. 1-12.
15. Ibid, IB File 120/41.
16. Ibid, Tsui Brain p. 354.
17. Ibid, Tsui Brain p. 354.
18. Ibid I.B. File: 120/ 41.
19. I.B.File No-120/41(1), Prof. Tan Yunshan, West Bengal State Archives.

20. This anniversary is popularly known as double tenth day celebration because it was celebrated on tenth day of October.
21. Report on the Political situation and Labour Unrest, 1929
22. op.cit., Tsui Brain: p. 356.
23. Ibid, I.B. File 120/41.
24. Ibid, I.B. File 120/41.
25. I.B. File No. 236/39(12), The Chinese in India. West Bengal State Archives.
26. Ibid, I.B. File: 236/39(12).
27. Tan-Yunshan (1944), *China-India and the war,* China Press, Princeep Street Calcutta. p. 23.
28. Ibid. I.B. File 120/41.
29. I.B. File No-195/44, Chinese Peoples Foreign Relation Association, West Bengal State Archives.
30. Ibid, I.B. File No-120/41(1).
31. Ibid, I.B. File: 120/41(1).
32. Taichi Tao and members of his good will mission visited all the important places of Buddhist Pilgrimage and had meeting with important Indian leaders. He was accompanied by Prof. Tan throughout the tour in India.
33. Ibid, I.B.File 120/41(1).
34. I.B. File No:1398/43.
35. Ibid, I.B. File 120/41.
36. Ibid, I.B. File 120/41(1).
37. Op. cit., Tan-Yunshan pp. 27-29.
38. Ibid, I.B.File No-120/41(1).
39. op. cit., Hung.
40. Ibid, I.B. File 12/41 (1)".
41. I.B. File- 2312-49 (1).
42. I.B. File-239/39(12).
43. Ibid, I.B. File 120/41.
44. Ibid, I.B. File 120/41.
45. Ibid, I.B. File 120/41.

Exploring Santal Interface with Nature and Culture

Pradip Chattopadhyay

The interaction between nature and culture is central to any discourse on environment. However, concern for environment in recent times is believed to have originated from the perceived ecological crisis that seems to threaten human civilization.[1] Notwithstanding this newly emerged concern for the protection of environment, the relationship between man and nature and its celebration has been going on in human societies for ages. However, the pace with which human society has developed over the last few centuries (aided and abetted by progress in science and technology and spread of the processes of urbanization and industrialization) has resulted in casting a shadow on this relationship between man and nature existed in the past. A faint glimpse of this relationship, however, may be discernible in the tribal societies in modern times as tribal people are reported to have retained many of their past beliefs and practices even today.[2] Also the rate of their transformation as well as evolution to modernity is believed to have been slow in comparison to the caste society. Indeed, for generations the tribals had shunned external influence and remained content with their peripheral existence. Throughout the ancient and medieval periods tribals had virtually stayed marginalized from the mainstream and their exposure to the forces of modernization and change only began with the advent of the colonial rule. Thus, in many respects tribal world view and perceptions of environment are not only distinct but also may be said to be the representative of the past notion of people about nature and culture.

There existed in ancient India the ethos of worshipping mountains, rivers, forests and animals. The inhabitants of the Indus region worshipped gods in the form of trees, animals and human beings. Harappan people looked upon the earth as a fertility goddess and worshipped her in the same manner as the Egyptians worshipped Nile goddesses Isis. Animals were worshipped in Harappan times and many of them were seen as represented on the seals. A male deity on a seal is surrounded by an elephant, a deer, a rhinoceros and a buffalo.[3] At his feet appear two deer. The four animals surrounding the deity look towards the four directions of the earth. The protection of elephants became a serious business during the time of the Mauryas. The Arthasastra mentions about the rules for protecting elephant forests.[4] Other types of forests are also preserved for animals and for protection of special species of trees. Forests always occupied a place of distinction in ancient India as they were considered to be the abodes of pantheon of gods and goddesses. In fact this tradition of worshipping nature is also visible in tribal societies.

Social scientists across disciplines have developed a number of analytical frameworks for defining the relationship between the tribals and their natural environment. Tribals have been defined as an ethnic category sharing a distinct kind of relationship with nature and they have also been delineated as backward and living at different stages of evolution. Recent revisionist scholars have tended to rewrite tribal culture as somewhat inseparable from its ecological settings and have criticized the colonial discourse for overdrawing the separation between forested landscape and livelihood patterns including agricultural relations of the tribals.[5] Even today, tribal societies represent exemplary dependence on nature for their culture and survival. It is said that the identity of the Adivasis is closely linked to the natural resources and the environment amidst which they live. Land (jamin), forests (jungle) and water (jal) are the main components of their survival which are also synonymous of their identity. Environmental interests and aspects are believed to have a direct bearing on many of the socio-religious beliefs and practices in tribal societies. Their round- the-year engagements in agricultural works, in gathering fruits and other essentials from forests, hunting and healing practices including celebration of fairs and festivals bear testimony to their relationship with nature. Besides, there are other issues which bear a direct reflection to tribal notion of environment. This study seeks to examine some of these beliefs and practices of the Santals in the past where their notion of environment appears to be more direct and distinctive.

Sentiments for Land & Forest

Santhals, for example, lived amid nature, surrounded by hills, forests, rivers and other natural manifestations. These elements provided them their sources of sustenance and also constituted an integral part of their culture. In fact, all the early narratives of colonial ethnographers and administrators have harped on this issue in no uncertain terms that Santhal settlements had developed with natural defenses all around. 'The Sonthal villages border those in the Sonthal Parganas and are situated in the narrow strip of broken high country west of the East Indian Railway, lying between the hills of the Sonthal Parganas, which approach the Birbhum border on the one side and the alluvial soil of the plains proper on the other. Where these hills recede from the border as in the South west of Murarai thana there are practically no Sonthal villages.'[6] Thus, their fascination for hills, forests and soil, particularly, laterite soil[7] as essential components for developing settlements was noted by early colonial ethnographers. In fact, all the past symbols of Santhal identity like gods and goddesses, totem[8] and tattoos, fairs and festivals, including numerous other beliefs and practices, were related to nature. So nature not only provided the context but also acted as an important variable for the formation of Santhal identity. Any change taking place in the physical atmosphere of the region is, therefore, bound to impact upon their views and values of life.

The Santhals used to nourish a special sentiment for land, it being regarded as synonymous of their identity. The loss of land meant the loss of identity to them. 'The traditional land base holds an important symbolic and emotional meaning for them as the repository of ancestral remains (Sasans), clan origin sites and other sacred features important to their religious system.'[9] The land system of the Santhals modeled on their traditional ideas and beliefs was fundamentally different from the agrarian system and structure of their non-tribal brethren. When the land was first reclaimed, the manjhi or the village headman acted as the sole spokesman for the entire village and engaged in a settlement with the superior landlord in relation to land rent. After consultation with his co-villagers, he agreed to pay a fixed amount of rent, which he collected from all the cultivators of the village. The headman then distributed the land among his co–villagers, making them responsible for the rent to be paid as per settlement. The headman too had to pay his share of rent for the land he held. He was however given a portion of the village land, around two to four bighas, in addition to his own share of land (nij jote), which he held rent-free. Such lands were called man/khem lands. But the headman, as also the other officials of the village who held man/khem lands by virtue of their position, could not claim any special privilege.[10] Thus, it was not a farming system in the ordinary sense of the term because the Santhal *mustagir* or headman/ farmer did not derive any profit. He was merely a rent-collecting individual and one among equals. Further, as the settlement was made verbally, it lacked the defined contractual character of the ordinary system.[11]

Like land the Santhals also cherished a sentiment for forests. In most cases they cleared forests before establishing villages. But they only cleared as much forests as they needed for setting up villages or creating agricultural land. Also trees were sometimes cut down for acquiring fuel-wood or building houses. Before the advent of the British, the Santhals used to enjoy customary rights over forests. The place in the forest thick in Sal and Mahua trees was earmarked by them as a *sacred grove*. The Santhals regarded this place as sacred and inviolable and the entire vegetation of the place was protected from encroachment. Forests not only played an important role in the economic life of the Santhals but also provided materials for their magico-religious beliefs and practices including health care. The Santhals had a profound knowledge of several medicinal plants and herbs which helped them to maintain their physical well being. Indeed, forests also constituted an integral part of their nature-worship. Hills, forests and rivers usually acted as natural defenses for their villages. Thus, the life of the Santhals in the past was nature-oriented and the whole gamut of magico-religious beliefs and practices including festivals were in a sense aimed at celebrating their relationship with nature.

Myth relating to Earth's Creation

Santal creation narratives[12] contain references to different elements of nature and their role in creating this earth as well as the stages that preceded the emergence of mankind. It is said that at the beginning there was only water and below the water was the earth. Then aquatic plants and animals came into being. The legend says, then *Thakur Jiu* at first decided to create human beings of clay. But before he could infuse life into them the horse sin *sadom*, (which had been kept close) trampled them. Then *Thakur Jiu* decided to make birds so that they would remain relatively free from getting killed or trampled upon by other creatures. He therefore made birds *Has* and *Hasil* from material scalding off his chest. The birds came to life as soon as *Thakur Jiu* blew into them and they immediately flew away. But they had nowhere to sit and take rest since there was water all around. So, after a while they came down and sat on *Thakur Jiu*'s hands. Meanwhile the horse felt thirsty and began drinking water. While drinking water it left some froth from his mouth in the water. It floated and produced more foam on the water. *Thakur Jiu* told the birds to go and sit on the foam which they did but soon they complained that though they could roam free by sitting on the foam water but they had noting to eat. Hearing this *Thakur Jiu* called upon all his aquatic animals that he had created earlier, namely, the alligator, the lobster, the raghop boar fish, stone crab, earth worm one by one asking them if they could collect earth from down the bottom of the sea. All had failed except earth worm. Then *Thakur Jiu* leveled the earth with harrow. 'While harrowing, the earth got heaped up in some places, these became mountains. When the earth was put in order the floating foam of the water got stuck to the earth'. On this foam thakur sowed mauricatus *seed* (Sirom) and then further sowed various grass and trees. Thus forests came into being. The birds, created earlier now could rest and build nests on trees. Soon the birds lay two eggs on nests. 'After some days from those two eggs emerged two human beings one boy and a girl'. As the two human beings were growing the anxiety of the birds also kept growing concerning where to keep these two.' The birds then started flying at the advice of *Thakur Jiu* in search of proper place for the human beings. They flew towards the place where the sun sets taking the human beings on their back and landed in Hihiri Pipiri. The birds then became untraceable. The human beings came to be known as Pilchu Haram and Pilchu Budhi. Soon they met Lita who claimed to be their grandfather. Lita then taught them the art of preparing liquor and asked them to drink it after offering a part of it to their god Marang Buru. Thus they became intoxicated and at night slept together involved in procreation. In the morning they felt ashamed of their bodies and covered them with the leaves of banyan tree. In course of time they got seven sons and daughters. The tradition goes on telling how the community grew, how the first generation of the community was destroyed by *Thakur Jiu* by fire from heaven because of their sin, how one pair survived the disaster and how the next generation grew up and wandered from place to place in the past, etc.

The narrative mentioned above is popularly known as Skrefsrud's version of Santal creation narrative which is said to have been taken down by Rev. L.O. Skrefsrud in 1870-1871 from an old guru named Kolean Guru. It is contained in the Santali book *Horkoren Mare Hapramko Reak Katha*. In addition to this, another version of the same is also available published by Rev. A. Campbell entitled *Santal Tradition*. The essence of the story in both the versions is more or less the same except a minor change in character and a more detailed delineation of the growing up of early human beings featuring in Campbell's version.

In this narrative the belief of Santal ancestors on *Thakur Jiu*'s role in creating this earth and human beings is clearly pronounced. Successive stages of creation beginning with water to aquatic plants and animals, to birds and finally the creation of human beings is clearly spelled out which bear a close resemblance with creation narratives of other traditions. In fact these narratives also indicate how the minds of past people used to work pertaining to nature and its various manifestations paving the way for the belief that all creations in this earth followed the divine wish and were united in a chain system sharing essential link with each other. Human beings were thus regarded as a part of the process of the same divine creation that also witnessed creation of water, earth, forests, aquatic animals and birds. The only difference, however, is that mankind perhaps emerged only at the end of this creation process to be preceded by all other living or non-living organisms. Thus, human beings in Santal creation narratives were not assigned any special position of respect or recognition for their intellectual calibre, thinking faculty and ethical supremacy and were merely treated as one among the other creations of god. This creation tradition of the Santals, it is clear, stands in contradiction to the creation narratives of caste people as they attach much greater importance to the agency of human beings in the kingdom of God. Indeed this approach of the Santals has imparted among them not only a sense of gratitude and respect towards nature but also has bred a sense of awe and fear for supernatural forces capable of causing death and devastation if hurt or displeased. This very approach to nature may also be said to have laid the foundations for all their socio-religious beliefs and practices.

Sacred Grove

The existence of the notion of sacred or holy grove in tribal culture may be interpreted as an indigenous way of preserving forests or at least a part of it, dotted with rare varieties of trees, scrubs, herbs and plants that have been revered by tribals through ages. The groves have always been considered to have links with certain cults and the entire vegetation in the grove surrounding that cult is regarded as sacred and inviolable. 'No vegetable matter, not even dead wood would be removed from the grove without incurring the wrath of the gods.[13] The only possible exception was fallen fruit that may be gathered.' However the groves seldom appear to be totemic in origin since no specific sacred tree species need be present in a sacred grove but it can be said that groves served to create proper setting for the cult rites.[14] 'Koshambi mentions the occurrence of groves among mother goddesses of the Atonga tribe of West Africa in which secret rites of the cult are performed by a sisterhood of priestesses. Any man entering the grove by accident is required to join the sisterhood and to dress and live like a woman for the rest of his life. There is a similar tale in Indian mythology of Manu's son Ila who entered the grove of the mother goddess Parvati by mistake and was transformed into a woman.'[15] Among other taboos denial of accessibility to males in the groves is significant.

In Santal culture groves appeared as a sacred place of worship for only the male members of the villages. Such groves were also storehouse of many plant species with medicinal value absent from the entire region. Forests of Bankura and Midnapore are full of sal and segun (teak) trees and the holy groves of the Santals contain these trees in abundance. Taboos and stories are in wide circulation relating to groves. It is said that attempts by individuals to cut down trees or to hunt animals in the groves have often resulted in death or severe injury of the encroachers. This lends credulance to the belief that 'the protection extended to the vegetation in the grove by the reigning deity is, or at least used to be, quite absolute.'[16]

Religious Beliefs & Practices

Religious beliefs and practices also constituted important elements of the ethnic identity of the Santhals in the past. The religious world of the Santhals was comprised of hordes of *Bongas* and *Spirits*. These *Bongas* were believed to have control over various natural phenomena and calamities. So, the Santhals always tried to appease them through magical and religious practices. These *Bongas* were often worshipped and propitiated with the sacrifice of animals, offerings of rice beer and the blood of the sacrificed animal. The village tutelary spirits of the Santhals consisted of *Marang Buru, Morenko Turiko, Jaher Era, Gosal Era, Parganas Bonga* and *Manjhi Haram Bonga*.[17] Also the sun, the moon and other manifestations of nature had an important place in the Santhal pantheon. However, the nature of Santhal worship was primarily congregational and the approach-collective. The religious festivals of the Santhals spanning the year were closely connected with their agricultural activities. The most important of the festivals were *Soharae Sim, Baha, Erok Sim, Iri-Gundhi, Nawai* and *Janther*. Besides, other important festivals like *Karam, Jom Sim,* and *Mak More* were also important. Every festival had two aspects, one the magico–religious, which covered the sacrifice and offerings to appease the deity and the other, the recreational, which provides entertainment and enjoyment including drinking, dancing, singing etc.[18] Charulal Mukherjee has commented that, "It seems as if the very heart of the tribe beats in unison with the advent of these tribal events, for it is here that the Santal plunges into his primitive herd-life to worship the tribal deities, to sing the advent of the agricultural season, to make merry over a bumper crops and to ward off by magic, the pests that hinder the sweet and even flow of their common life."[19] In fact Santals in the past felt that various aspects of their economic life were needed to be guarded by appropriate ceremonials and rituals to the tribal deities, so that the beneficient may protect the harvest and the malevolent *Bongas* may be shorn of their malign influence. These sacrifices and libations to deities and ancestor-spirits are closely associated with all Santal public festivals. The life of the Santals in the past was threatened by natural calamities and disasters of various kinds. For example, there might be insufficient rain or too much of it. Locusts might eat up the corn grown and as the people look up to these baffling mysteries of existence, they look for confidence and want to secure good luck for themselves and their tribe. 'Through these festival the Santals wanted to establish a communion with the superhuman powers by first of all propitiating them with the hope that they in their benevolence may influence the destinies of the tribe at such turning points in the material life of the tribe.'[20]

Healing Practices and Superstitions

Traditional healing practices and associated superstitions were also in many ways related to their perception about natural environment. Earlier the belief was that the diseases and calamities occurred due to god's wrath and influence of evil spirits. Anything that disturbs the normal course of life, be it in the form of sickness, disease or a natural calamity was conceived as unnatural by the Santals. According to P.O. Bodding,[21] Santals suffered from many peculiar ideas about these evil spirits and their mode of operation. They considered that natural objects like, trees, hillocks etc., could be 'possessed' by evil spirits but it was not possible to know in advance which tree hillock or physical object would be possessed by an evil bonga. However, it was believed that if a boy falls down after climbing up a tree and suffers an injury, it was indicative of the tree being possessed by an evil spirit. Such a tree then became an object of worship. If for some reasons the tree dried up, the popular interpretation was that the tree could not stand the impact of the evil bonga possessing it. Sitakant Mahapatra[22] has explained that there is noting called 'accident' in the life of the Santals. Whenever they faced accidents like drowning in a stream, snake-bitting or devouring by a tiger resulting in death or perpetual maiming, they attributed them to 'unnatural situations.'

Santals accepted death as ordained by the Marangburu. The issue of death never seemed to bother them in the past. Like most other primitive communities, they also displayed lack of obsession with regard to death as they were more concerned about the pleasure and pains of life and the joys and sorrows of daily existence. Of course, they too suffered from pathos and bewilderment with the death of their near and dear ones but death appeared to them as something that they could not do much against. Probably due to their total surrender to the inevitability of death the spirit to enjoy present life reigned supreme in them.[23] Santals belonging to the present generation may differ from this attitude but it is true that their counterparts in the past hardly had any fear about death or the nagging old age. Suicide was also extremely rare among them in the past.

The most striking aspect of the traditional Santal attitude towards health was their belief in the role of supernatural forces in maintaining physical well being including existence on the earth. This notion had indeed blurred their real awareness about pain or disease and instead prepared them to accept or tolerate pain as a part of earthly existence. Not only that even sufferings and miseries were considered as necessary in the purificatory process to be recompensed in the next life. This culture of attributing mishaps and misfortunes to divine providence had in fact dented Santal initiatives to seek a realistic approach to disease and death.[24]

Witchcraft existed as an integral part of the religio-magical beliefs of the Santals in the past. A.B. Chowdhuri has mentioned that the extent of the problem of witch-killing including tortures of varying degrees practiced by the Santals has been very widespread in West Bengal as well as in other states.[25] The Santal belief in witchcraft is believed to have originated from their respect for and fear of the Bongas. Among the Santals, the principal element in the assumption of supernatural power was the concept of the Bongas, the power that controlled nature. Earlier the Santals believed that these Bongas, at times, could become wrathful and make life miserable. The witches had liaison with these spirits or Bongas and therefore, they also had the power to cause harm to man.[26] This belief in the malevolent Bongas, and the possible relationship between the witches and these Bongas had, in fact, made the phenomenon of witchcraft in Santal society very difficult to bear. Though Santals in general did not always believe in wrathful Bongas since they had been worshipping these Bongas for centuries, some of them at least, shared the idea that the witches or others might have actually turned the Bongas against them and that only the witch-doctors could identify such witches.[27] In the Santal society there were witch-doctors known as ojhas or jangurus who were in charge of warding off evil bongas or spirits by worshipping gods, observing rituals, making sacrifices and performing religio-magical practices.

Witches role as Shamans or traditional healers is also much talked about issue in present times. Riane Eisler has commented that witches were traditional healers witch accusations were aimed at discrediting the healing knowledge of women. Studies from different regions in India also hint at women's shamanistic roles. Verrier Elwin, for example, talks about Saora women's shamanism and that they were custodians of black magic and had unrivalled knowledge of herbs and plants. Skaria says dakans were often thought to be good at gathering. In Chotanagpur the relationship of women with nature and forests and their knowledge of roots, herbs and plants were quite established in the community domain and belief system.[28]

Thus Santal views relating to the causes of death and disease may be categorized into three heads – the natural, the malign and the divine. The remedy for natural illness or sickness would be sought in herbal medicines while those caused by malevolent bongas/spirits or withches would be addressed through incantations, charms and sacrifices administered by the ojhas or jangurus. A third category that caused death and devastation in larger scale was attributed to gods and goddesses and elaborate arrangements to propitiate were in place in the society of the Santals.[29]

Understanding tribal perception of nature is thus significant to understand the approach of the past people to natural environment. Indeed, it was this perception that had shaped their world-view, including ideas and attitudes to life. The distinctive element in it was the recognition that nature was a domain of God, an area of God's manifestation in all its flora and fauna. Accordingly, dependence on nature for survival and economic use of natural resources became an integral part of their religo-cultural ethos. However, this ethos has undergone changes with the passage of time and with the achievement of progress in science and technology. The spread of the processes of industrialization and urbanization all over the world and the consequent material advancement that came alongside has made men overconfident to randomly exploit nature, the ill effect of which has resulted in frequent visits of natural calamities like cyclone, tsunami, flood and earthquake.

Notes and References

1. Debates are widespread pertaining to interaction between nature and culture. However debates on sustainable or eco-friendly development or human engagement in industrialization and urbanization processes at the cost of nature have attracted attention most in recent times.
2. D.D. Koshambi has remarked in his essay entitled 'The Contribution of D.D. Koshambi to Indology', in Romila Thapar (ed.) *Interpreting Early India* , Oxford, 1992, p. 91, that 'historian in India was in a particularly happy position since so much of the past survives in the present ... the survival within different social layers of many forms that allow the reconstruction of totally diverse earlier stages.'
3. R.S. Sharma, *Ancient India,* NCERT, 1980, p. 40.
4. Ranjan Chakrabarti (ed.), *Situating Environmental History,* New Delhi, Manohar, 2007, p. 13.
5. A. Agarwal and K. Sivaramkrishnan (2001), *Social Nature: Resources, Representations, and Rule in India,* Delhi, OUP, 2001, p. 2.
6. M.C. McAlpin, *Report on the Condition of the Sonthals of Bankura, Birbhum, Midnapore and North Balasore,* Calcutta, Firma KLM, 1981, p. 4.
7. Ibid, p. 6.
8. Charulal Mukherjea in his book *The Santals,* Calcutta, A. Mukherjee & Company Pvt. Ltd, 1962 shows p. 108, shows that clans are totemistic. Certain relationships exist between him and some physical phenomena or some tangible objects such as an animal, a bird or even some plant or grass. Thus, Murmus revere the Nilgai, Hansdak hold sacred the duck, Marandis salute if they happen to cut Marandi grass. The general rule is that a member of the same totem will never kill or hurt the object he derives his name from nor will he tolerate intermarriage within the clan.
9. Mathew Areeparampil, *Struggle for Swaraj,* Chaibasa, Tribal Research & Training Centre, 2002, p. 7.
10. A.K. Banerjee, *West Bengal District Gazetteers, Bankura,* Calcutta: 1968, p. 170.
11. Ibid, p. 170.
12. T. Hembrom, *The Santals,* Calcutta, Punthi Pustak, 1996, pp. 82-87.
13. Madhav Gadgil & V.D. Vartak, 'The Sacred Use of Nature', in Ramachandra Guha (ed.), *Social Ecology,* OUP, 1994, p. 88.
14. Ibid., p. 85.
15. Quoted from Ibid, p. 85.

16. Ibid, p. 87.
17. A.K Das, U.K. Roy, and S.K. Basu, *To be with Santals*, SC & ST Dept. Calcutta: Govt. of West Bengal, 1977, p. 49.
18. Ibid, p. 59.
19. Charulal Mukherjee, *The Santals*, A. Mukherjee & Co. 1962, p. 232.
20. Ibid., p. 271.
21. P.O. Bodding, *The Santals and Disease*, Calcutta, Royal Asiatic Society of Bengal, 1925.
22. Sitakant Mahapatra, *Modernization and Ritual*, OUP, 1986, p. 92.
23. Ibid, p. 91.
24. Ibid., p. 91.
25. A.B. Chadhuri, *Witch Killings Amongst Santals*, New Delhi, Asia Publishing House, 1984, p. 10.
26. Pradip Bhattacharya, *Witchcraft Among the Santals*, Calcutta, Liberal Association for Movement of People (LAMP), 1994, p. 10.
27. Ibid, p. 10.
28. Quoted from Shashank S. Sinha, 'Adivasis, Gender and the Evil Eye, The Construction(s) of Witches In Colonial Chotanagpur', in Biswamoy Pati (ed.), *Adivasis in Colonial India*, New Delhi, Orient Blackswan, 2013 p. 117.
29. David Hardiman, 'Knowledge of the Bhils and their Systems of Healing', in Biswamoy Pati (ed.), *Adivasis in Colonial India*, New Delhi, Orient Blackswan, 2013, pp. 312-313.

Contributors

1. SAHARA AHMED, Professor in the Department of History, Rabindra Bharati University
2. Lt. SRILATA CHATTERJEE, former Professor in the Department of History, Calcutta University
3. PRADIP CHATTOPADHYAY, Professor in the Department of History, Burdwan University
4. APARNA BANDYOPADHYAY, Associate Professor in the Department of History, Diamond Harbour Women's University,
5. DEBRAJ CHAKRABORTY, Assistant Professor in the Department of History, Berhampore Girls' College, Berhampore, Murshidabad
6. NIRMAL BANDYOPADHYAY, Assistant Teacher, Sodepur High School, Sodepur
7. BIDISHA CHAKRABORTY, Archivist at the State Archives of West Bengal
8. ARPITA BOSE, Assistant Professor in the Department of History, Durgapur Government College, Durgapur
9. SUMITA CHAKRABORTY, Ph.D. Scholar in the Department of History, Burdwan University

Editors:

1. Prof. Pradip Chattopadhyay is currently serving as Professor in the Department of History, the University of Burdwan.
2. Dr. Aparajita Dhar is Head of the Department of History the University of Burdwan.
3. Dr. Binata Sarkar is serving as Assistant Professor of History, the University of Burdwan